Love
That
Lasts

A Singles Guide to Finding a Great Mate

Dorothy Jongeward, Ph.D.
and Michele Raffin, M.M.S.

✳ The Crossing Press, Freedom, CA 95019

Acknowledgments

We express our gratitude to all the people who trusted us enough to share their secrets, sorrows, "lessons" and joys. Most of their tales taught us wisdom. Some charmed and entertained us. All warmed our hearts. We thank you.

We also extend our appreciation to the many test readers who gave us important feedback, constructive criticism and direction. We thank you.

Library of Congress Cataloging-in-Publication Data

Jongeward, Dorothy.
    Love that lasts : a singles guide to finding a great mate / by
Dorothy Jongeward, and Michele Raffin.
        p.   cm.
    Includes bibliographical references.
    ISBN 0-89594-590-8 (cloth). -- ISBN 0-89594-589-4 (pbk,)
    1. Mate selection. 2. Man-woman relationships. 3. Interpersonal
relations. I. Raffin, Michele. II. Title.
HQ801.J66 1993
646.7'7--dc20

                                            93-5282
                                             CIP

Dedication

We dedicate this book to our permanent partners, Tom and Wally, and to all the people who are serious about doing what it takes to have a long-lasting, challenging, loving, growing, committed relationship.

Michele makes a special dedication to Ruth Gross to fulfill a 30-year-old promise and to John McNeel who said that all it would take would be to change her view of herself and the world.

Dorothy makes a special dedication to all her family members, friends, clients and students who have been her greatest teachers.

Contents

Introduction

The handsome prince gazed down into the limpid eyes of the beautiful, young woman. He knew in an instant he was in love. She flushed. A thrill shivered its way through her slender body as she timidly raised her eyes to more fully meet his. Without a moment's hesitation she knew deep inside that she loved him beyond anything she'd ever known. Their hands touched. It was magic. They soon walked down the aisle and lived happily-ever-after.

Have you noticed that all good fairy tales seem to stop here? Jobs, bills, dishes, taking out the garbage, ironing, cleaning, the lawn, emergency rooms, camping out, laundry, toilet bowls, neighbors, PTA meetings, cooking—all these realities of life after the marriage ceremony don't make for exciting reading. Many of our own ideas about marriage are just as unrealistic. After all, most children hear over and over again how the prince rescued the poor damsel, how the damsel rescued the frog. The excitement is in the magic and in the chase. Is it any wonder that as adults, long after we put aside beliefs in the tooth fairy and Santa Claus, many of us continue to operate as if the promises of instant, forever-more love can be true if only we are just beautiful enough, strong enough, sacrificing enough, or brave enough?

Fairy tale illusions are just that—fairy tale illusions! The divorce statistics attest to the real situation. Since 1920, instead of happily-ever-after, while people continue to marry at the same rate, the divorce rate has tripled. Half of all marriages now end in divorce. Second marriages fail at the rate of six out of ten. While the breadwinner/homemaker model thrived between 1860 and 1920 (when it was historically a relatively new idea), fewer than 27 percent of the nation's over 90 million households now fit such a model.[1] Marriage is indeed a fragile institution. You may have experienced first-hand the real difficulty of "living happily-ever-after." However, we think you can get much closer—closer than you might believe at this moment—to a more realistic, happy, fulfilling and lasting relationship.

- *If* you are genuinely looking for a life partner, for a relationship that lasts;
- *If* you are willing to examine and give up the fairy tale model of romance in favor of conscious choices;
- *If* you are willing to take the risks and have the energy to put your feet down firmly on a new but proven path, *this book is meant for you.*

1

In these pages we share those qualities, ideas, secrets and ideals that are common to people who experience failure in relationships, learn from these failures, and then successfully enter into loving, lasting partnerships. People do need people. Those who are happy in relationships live longer, healthier lives, fulfill a sense of continuity with the human race, and are better able to face the daily provocations that force them to grow. However, the journey isn't easy—and it certainly isn't for everyone. There are many challenges and the road can be bumpy, but there is every reason to believe that you can enter into a permanent partnership that works for you.

Many singles who are unsuccessful at finding a mate think that just *meeting* someone is their biggest obstacle. This is not true. In Chapter 7, you'll find a way to meet as many new people as you wish. Here we outline the principles of Social Networking. We base these principles on the skills and techniques learned from successful executive search teams to find just the right person for a job opening. Social Network Parties are gatherings that produce a plethora of potential partners. What then is the toughest part? *Recognizing and feeling attracted to the right person—the person who is appropriate for you—is the trick.* That's also the reason that the system of Social Networking appears as late as it does in this book. You may very well need to take other steps first so that you don't fall into a trap just because you meet a pretty woman or a nice guy.

How did we arrive at the conclusion that finding a person whose chemistry clicks is only part of what is needed in order to ensure permanency? We asked the questions: What goes into a permanent partnership? What's different about those couples whose marriages continue to be satisfying? How did they find each other? How did they court? How did they select? How did they decide? Just what is it that people have to do and be in order to participate in an on-going relationship in which they are happy, committed, trusting, and able to love and be loved?

If you want to know about success, talk to successful people. That's exactly what we did. We listened to the stories of over 100 people who had been married for 15 to 50 years. From this group we selected 50 couples whose partners had been through failed relationships but now appeared to be extremely happy. We interviewed them in depth to discover any common threads.[2]

Surprisingly, there was remarkable similarity in the steps taken by each to reach a maturity level necessary for becoming successful permanent partners. The steps took insight, determination and effort. Each person's journey required making *significant internal changes*. When combined with Social Networking, these five steps make up the "Matching Process," that forms the heart of this book.

Successful people follow successful patterns. This is just as true for forming intimate relationships as it is for sports, career, health or any other aspect of life. The patterns that emerged from people's stories were consistent. Following their successful patterns will empower you not only to find your partner but also to become personally capable of lasting love—to *be* a permanent partner.

Step One challenges you to recognize the signs of a disturbed relationship. We call this "relationsickness," putting the emphasis only on those issues which shape relationships. It encourages you to get yourself ready for a mature partnership by healing any wounds that deter you now. It looks at some of the causes of people's inabilities to make commitments, to enjoy intimacy and to trust. It suggests, if necessary, that you select a mode of healing. Step Two urges you to clarify what you want. Step Three discusses wholeness and offers insight into learning from your projections. Step Four explains Social Networking and shows you how to make an effective search for the right person. And Step Five asks you to let go, open yourself and allow "fate" to take its course. Other chapters focus on what it means and what it takes to actually be a permanent partner. Couples share what gives them the edge in maintaining relationships in which they are happy, growing, accepting, committed, trusting, and able to give and receive love—which is what a healthy permanent partnership offers. With each step you will find exercises, questions and questionnaires that will enhance the speed and effectiveness of your quest. Since the stakes are high, we hope these steps will save you the time, effort, and frustration inherent in a trial-and-error method.

In addition to the five-step Matching Process just described, we also uncovered additional basic principles to consider in your search for a love that endures. While these principles speak the truth, they seem to go against conventional wisdom:

- Meeting potential partners is relatively easy.
- Being a permanent partner is extremely challenging.
- You do not need to make external changes to be more attractive to members of the opposite sex.
- But you may need to *make significant internal changes to be more attractive to yourself.*

Successful partnerships are made up of confident, successful people. The glow of self-esteem radiates the right stuff for the right reasons—reasons far more profound than being thinner, richer, wittier, and the many other externals on which frustrated singles often focus. That inner glow is an irresistible attraction.

We hope to help you get to your core—that part of your being that is loving, caring, accepting, non-judgmental, and, above all, happy. What better way to experience this essential essence of yourself than in a happy, lasting relationship?

ENDNOTES

1. See *Newsweek*, Winter/Spring 1990, "The 21st Century Family."

2. Appendix A gives you more details about the research project and case histories.

Chapter 1

You Can Find a
Permanent Partner

Some men see things as they are and say 'Why?' I dream things that never were, and say, 'Why not?'

George Bernard Shaw

"Don't worry. You'll get a glimpse of your husband in the morning at the ceremony. It'll be a good match."

"You've been betrothed to your future bride since she was six months old. You'll marry her when she is 13."

"Sally, just wait until you meet Harry. He's marvelous! He's the perfect match for you and I've looked over at least 30 other fellows."

Arranged marriages were once common in Asia and in Europe, and many societies still hold to the practice. In some societies, matchmakers are responsible for introducing prospective mates by finding single men and women, assessing their suitability and introducing potential partners. Sometimes parents, family members, priests or political leaders play this role.

In arranged marriages there was a contract between families, not between individuals. The family looked for another family of equal rank and good financial reputation, with no hereditary diseases. The families increased their financial or social standings sometimes welding two kingdoms together through the marriage bed. Divorce was impossible or at least rare. A disappointing wife to a king was banished to a nunnery or the chopping block. No one worried about couples staying together or whether or not they were happy. A happy marriage is a relatively new concept. The old rule was the couple had to stay together—forever. After all, as it is sung out in *Fiddler on the Roof*, "It's *Tradition!*" Most of the world still puts little trust in young people having the good sense and skills to do their own matchmaking. A traditional Japanese saying warns, "Arranged marriages start out cold and get hot, whereas love matches start out hot and grow cold."[1] Even so, no matter how primitive or sophisticated the culture, the phenomenon of "falling in love" has been with us a long time.

Romantic Love and Divorce

Only a few nations such as the United States, Western Europe and Polynesia, possess or have possessed in the past the notion that falling in love is a highly desirable prerequisite for courtship and marriage. Indeed, romantic love as a component in marriage selection is a fairly recent innovation.

Getting people to stay married has posed a problem to societies for centuries. Those in power recognized the difficulty in keeping love alive. As a consequence, there is a long history of pressure being applied to couples (particularly to women) by governments, religious institutions, cultures and families to force them to stay married. With these constraints now removed and with couples relying on romantic love to hold their relationship in place, many find that there is much more to lasting love than instant attraction and bells and tingles. Relationships demand not only our love and our chemistry but our maturity, skills, intentions and determination. In the real world, lasting love without work, attention and growth is rare indeed.

To modern eyes, the old systems appear cold, unrealistic and unnatural. After all, we are freedom-loving, independent individuals who want to control our own destinies. We want to choose a mate by falling in love and just having it all "happen." In fact, we want it to happen *effortlessly*. This common illusion pervades our culture. "Once you find your mate, it's smooth sailing," is a powerful but incorrect notion. Dr. M. Scott Peck observes that the myth of romantic love is a dreadful lie. "Perhaps it is a necessary lie in that it ensures the survival of the species by its encouragement and seeming validation of the falling-in-love experience that traps us into marriage. But, as a psychiatrist, I weep in my heart almost daily for the ghastly confusion and suffering that this myth fosters. Millions of people waste vast amounts of energy desperately and futilely attempting to make the reality of their lives conform to the unreality of the myth."[2]

Myth or no, we would never consider giving up choosing our own mates, and rightly so—it is one of the most important decisions of our lives and it has become one of our most treasured freedoms. However, the ultimate problem with freedom is that it carries with it a great load of responsibility. We have the responsibility for making many important choices without a clear picture of the consequences. In a sense, we have taken on the responsibility for being our own matchmakers with neither the experience nor the training to be proficient at it. Many of us aspire to make a commitment that lasts a lifetime, but, judging by the statistics, we don't know how.

The prospects for today's marriages are dim. People who form satisfying, lifelong partnerships are definitely in the minority. Neither instruction manual nor guarantee comes with the marriage ceremony. While we certainly can grow through negative experiences, dealing with the consequences of divorce is usually grim, costly, often long lasting, and sometimes even dangerous. We've failed. We've made a losing choice. We suffer pain through separation from children, loss of friends, loss of property and even loss of self-esteem. The personal costs are high, and society pays a price, too.

Blocks to Permanent Partnerships

Why is finding and being a permanent partner so difficult? Why aren't relationships and modern marriage working well? These are complex questions. However, in addition to the myth of romantic love, there are five contributing factors that greatly impact both the search for a partner and family stability: 1) At the top of the list is the high number of people who have had negative experiences, often in childhood, which impair their capacity for intimacy; 2) In our complex culture it is difficult to know when we are mature enough to be ready for adult responsibilities; 3) It takes many years to prepare for a rewarding career; 4) Our priorities most are often confused; 5) The evolving egalitarian relationship between men and women challenges our traditional beliefs and attitudes and prods us to create a new vision for the future. Is it any wonder that in the midst of so many social pressures, issues and changes, we mortals make wrong choices?

Intimacy is critical for a healthy marital partnership, yet millions of people feel inhibited from attaining it. Contributing to this is the high incidence of child neglect, abuse and molestation which leaves lasting emotional scars on many psyches. Such scars must be healed and overcome to regain the human capacity for intimacy and trust. Many people have never experienced a positive model. Family violence is common. Estimates report that each year three to four million women experience violence in their homes. A woman is being beaten somewhere every few seconds and 3,000 to 4,000 women are beaten to death by a partner every year.[3] Such unhappiness is passed on from generation to generation, even though the cycle can be stopped in one.

Ancient societies (and primitive ones even today) knew the power and function of rituals to set important benchmarks in a person's life. Strenuous, often secret, initiatory rites gave men and women a point in time when they knew clearly they were adults and took their place in the community as responsible members. However, rites of passage don't exist for most of us today. While this gives us great freedom, the deep human need for marking our transitions can be manifested in such places as street gangs, corporate headquarters, emergency rooms, and ivory towers. This omission results in many of us playing in an immature and inexperienced way at sex and marriage, often leading to children rearing children, people growing apart, family instability and even violence.

Our bodies reach puberty at an increasingly early age. However, the length of time needed to become educated and trained for an occupation grows longer and longer. Our complex society pushes adolescence well into the 20's and 30's. As a result, many people make poor choices about sexuality and marriage during this confusing and difficult time.

In addition, our timing tends to be backward. We look for our true love, then figure out how we want to live the rest of our lives. It makes much more sense to re-evaluate our priorities so that we grow into full adulthood, set our course in life and *then* find the right companion to journey with us. Getting this backward leads to much misery—as you may have experienced.

To add to the complexities, we are in the midst of a sex-role transition. Some see it as a gender crisis. As women emerge to assume greater economic and political responsibility, and as men are challenged to accept more responsibility for family life, traditional roles and ways of relating give way. Both men and women are re-defining what a permanent partnership really means. This new sense of partnership requires full maturation. It takes emotionally mature people to steer a lifelong partnership on a healthy course and to raise the next generation. For better or worse, we are in the position of being our own matchmakers. But what's even more exciting? We are at the forefront of a relatively new human experience! Crises most frequently precede transformation, and in all crises lay the potential for both danger and opportunity. According to chaos theory, things often appear to fall apart before they fall together again in new configurations.

Motives for Marriage Are Changing

Motives for modern marriage are quite different from those of the past. People used to need marriage partners for survival. It took teamwork to get food on the table and a roof overhead. Such couples often grew to have great affection for each other—but there was no guarantee. No longer do we marry for survival. We want a whole lot more. And we want it almost as instantaneously and miraculously as we push the buttons on our remote control to find our favorite programs on TV. We want love, family, personal fulfillment, monetary success, material comforts, emotional fulfillment, mutual growth *and* happiness: And that is a tall order for mere mortals.

This book is about just that—tall orders. It seeks to show a way to achieve all that you want in a lasting, permanent relationship. Permanent partnerships are as hard to define as "love." No description covers every facet of this precious commodity. There is so much to explore.

Permanent Partnership

Permanent means everlasting. It is the "until death do us part" portion of the marriage vow. One woman who heard the term declared, "Who needs a permanent partner? I've been in this miserable relationship for nearly 30 years!" That's not quite what we're talking about. Permanent partnership means not only long lasting but also continuing vitality. More than perpetual existence, it implies ongoing vibrancy and positive energy. Permanent is not used in the sense of never-changing, always being the same. On the contrary, the best way to ensure permanency is to build mechanisms into a relationship which facilitate continuous growth and change. *Anything alive is in constant flux!* There is a Zen saying: "You can never step twice into the same stream."

With couples, permanent does not mean fixed or stagnant. Instead, it means to exist for a long, indefinite period, taking the future in stride. It means that couples weather unforeseeable future events in ways appropriate to the severity of the storm. They meet adverse conditions with the harmony and synergy of a team effort. Permanent partners learn to flex and flow with life's events.

In business, a partnership means "sharing in the risks and in the profits." Much the same is involved in a marriage partnership. There are times that are definitely "for better or for worse." We risk the unknown, the unpredictable and even tragic events which can happen. To be a partner is to share and partake—both give and receive. There is an implication in the word "partnership" not only of give-and-take but, in a much larger sense, of equality and justice. Equality doesn't mean that both partners give and receive equally everyday— there is no daily scorecard. In the long run, partnerships can't be maintained in one-up/one-down or win/lose relationships. Such relationships only breed resentments, lack of growth and mental stress. Both partners need to have individual needs as well as team needs met. Putting aside one partner's needs to meet the other partner's needs is a two-way street.

Permanent partners share power. Both receive and dispense justice in the relationship. One does not exist at the expense of the other. They make decisions equally as their real talents allow. When they delegate decisions to one or the other, it's by mutual consent. They change and grow as naturally and smoothly as possible, but always in the best interests of both people. Shared power is really a key ingredient to egalitarian relationships.

As Kahlil Gibran wrote long ago in *The Prophet*:

"Give your hearts, but not into each others keeping.
For only the hand of Life can contain your hearts.
And stand together yet not too near together:
For the pillars of the temple stand apart,
And the oak tree and the cypress grow not in each other's shadow."[4]

The signs that a person is a true permanent partner candidate usually exist from the very beginning of the relationship. Over and over again, successful partners described their spouses in a similar fashion. Rather than being manipulative, coercive, destructive, distant, irresponsible, or unpredictable, they found them:

positive—honest, courteous, nurturing;
consistent—predictable, accountable;
compatible—having enough fundamental beliefs, interests and goals in common to make the merger of two lives possible;
trustworthy—committed to and capable of intimacy.

Clues to Quality Permanent Partners

We all know these characteristics are not easy to come by. On the other hand, there are clues that people who later form successful partnerships have learned to watch for and take seriously. In fact, several major clues to quality permanent partnerships emerged from our interviews with well-matched couples. They testify to the fact that much deeper qualities than a date's occupation, looks, or make-of-car form the core of true partnership. How can you tell a good potential partner when you first get to know someone?

Clue #1: *The way you are treated while dating is the way you are likely to be treated always.* We all have both psychological and physical boundaries that are reasonable and that preserve our safety and self-esteem. If these boundaries are in any way violated by verbal or physical abuse, the relationship is unhealthy. This clue seems so obvious that it shouldn't even be listed. But, obvious or not, it is often ignored. If you find yourself having to make excuses for a person's behavior, it's a clue the person might be right for somebody other than you. If someone is always late, puts you down in front of others, makes promises that aren't kept, or borrows things that are never returned (like money), a red flag should go up. Worse yet, if someone shoves or hits you when frustrated, think twice before you ask for more. In fact, as a relationship develops, you may be in for worse treatment. The abuse of power in any relationship is a major flaw. What people actually do counts far more than what they say. Beware means "be aware." Keep your eyes and ears open because how you're treated now is how you are likely to be treated later.

Clue #2: *As a good indication of respect, observe the time and effort taken to mutually decide when physical involvement should develop.* Physical intimacy should never be coerced. Taking time to make mutual decisions recognizes individual standards and the importance of safe sex which demonstrates not only self-confidence, but also the importance of each other's feelings, values, health and standards. If caring and consideration are not there in the beginning, they may never be. While most of us would agree that chemistry is important, chemistry alone can lead us down the wrong path. Rather, look for a lasting passion generously mixed with a compassion that doesn't fizzle out when the excitement is over. You have to clarify your own standards and appreciate someone who honors them.

Clue #3: *Middle steps tell you how a relationship is growing.* If you have ever felt "burned" in the love department, you may need to pay special attention to letting a new relationship grow. Middle steps are the things you do together while taking the time and making the effort to let the relationship evolve. It could be as simple as trying something new together or having long talks. Men tend to relate better shoulder to shoulder while doing an activity. Women like to face a partner and talk. Such things as a dinner date, a walk in the woods or a fishing trip allow for both. These middle steps are for gathering information, learning about each other's personalities and interests, and developing mutual respect. They are part of developing trust and intimacy. Don't expect trust, intimacy and commitment to be there immediately. They grow in stages. If your date is consistently kind, considerate, courteous, generous—whatever is really important to you—but the bells don't ring right away, wait. The relationship may well deserve the time you devote to it. As a young accountant named Peter put it, "Instant intimacy, like instant coffee, is not as good as the correctly brewed variety." Even though it's rare, some people do indeed experience "love at first sight" that is genuine. However, most people need to be cautious and allow the trust and commitment that is part of getting to know each other evolve. Pushing too hard or too fast is a clue to lack of development and nurturing of the relationship. After all, you don't want to find yourself with someone you really don't know *after* the vows are taken—especially if this has happened to you before.

Clue #4: *Reciprocity, the ability to give and take, gives you a measure of the health of a relationship.* When a relationship is moving in the right direction, mutual caring, affection, problem solving, and nurturing become part of it. It is essential that both partners participate. For example, a typical pattern of people with a history of troubled relationships is to play fixed roles. One might provide all the thinking and leading, while the other person is consistently submissive. When one partner does most or all of the thinking, decision making and leading or is forced to "pretend," a warning light should flash. Danger! Danger! Remember that genuine partnerships, though not always exactly equal all of the time, tend to balance over time. Look for affection returned by affection, emotional sharing by emotional sharing, etc. Be aware if both of you can give and also receive and if you both can be nurturing. Be aware if control of situations is passed back and forth appropriately, depending on the situation, and who is most capable of handling it. Be aware if power is shared. Mutuality is the key. Good partnerships are mutual. Reflect on the impact of reciprocity in your past relationships and what your roles were.

Clue #5: *Being good friends, wanting to be with each other and wanting to share and do things together is a sign of a lasting relationship.* Look for a developing friendship. When you see a beautiful sunset, you think of the other person and wish you could share it. Sharing goes both ways and includes recreational activities, educational activities and cultural events. You are not just a dinner date. You start thinking of the person as a good friend, someone to go places with, someone to do things with, someone you can be honest with and bare your soul. In return, you are treated as a good friend.

Clue #6: *Communication patterns indicate whether or not a relationship has the potential for staying power, and whether or not you both have the skills to work out differences.* If you have ever worked as part of a team on any project, you know that certain rules of communication need to be followed or the team effort breaks down. There are four communication patterns that point to possible failure: 1) Signs of contempt often expressed through sarcastic remarks or facetiousness—wisecracks with a painful barb; 2) Becoming defensive which dramatically diminishes the chances of solving problems and clearing the air because, rather than dealing with the issues at hand, the communication degrades into attack and defense; 3) Being critical which puts people and their ideas down, stops creativity and can pull good feelings and energy down; 4) Withdrawing, whereby people stop contributing and turn away from straightforwardly facing issues that need to be brought out and talked over. These same communication patterns apply equally to personal teamwork. If you are spoken to with contempt; or if you are overly criticized; or, if in response to problems, there is defensiveness or withdrawal, you should recognize these signs as pulling apart, not together. Be wary.

Clue #7: *Being with this person enhances your sense of well-being. You feel energized rather than depleted.* Have you noticed that some people leave you feeling drained? The crux of this clue is to feel accepted simply for who you are. The person knows your reality and likes it. False flattery does not have you floating on cloud nine while setting yourself up for a big letdown. Instead, you feel comfortable with this person even with egg on your face. Pay attention to your feelings of self-esteem, your feelings of being solid and grounded, your sense of being accepted for who you are, your energy level. Don't be fooled by fantasy and flattery. Don't get yourself into a relationship where you feel compelled to act as if you are someone you are not. You may have already found that relationships can bring out the worst. Healthy relationships bring out the best.

Once you start watching for the elements of a healthy relationship and start taking important clues seriously, you can set your sights more clearly and realistically for a permanent partner. There are wonderful potential matches all around you. They're in the supermarkets, at political rallies, on planes, on the campus—anywhere people gather. Many people are looking for permanent partners. Right now an appropriate, delightful person who is ready to commit to a relationship is likely to be looking for you. The Matching Process will show you a way to get together.

The Five-Step Matching Process

The Matching Process has five critical steps. Each step has a chapter or two devoted to it which describes the step and ways to make it work for you. To find your permanent partner you must:

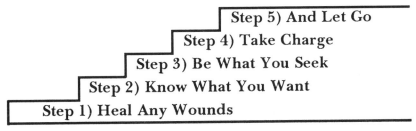

Step 5) And Let Go
Step 4) Take Charge
Step 3) Be What You Seek
Step 2) Know What You Want
Step 1) Heal Any Wounds

All but Step Four focus on getting you prepared for a new and successful match. Step Four tells you how to arrange special gatherings of special people. We call this process Social Networking. It is designed to help you in your search for a winning love match. However, most of the work you must do involves getting yourself ready to attract and be attracted to a partner appropriate for you. These steps can be tiny shuffles or wide strides, depending on how much energy you put into them. However, unlike conventional steps, if you skip over some of them, you will not reach your goal any sooner. Treat each step like a fine meal, a wonderful massage, or a memorable journey. Savor each one slowly and completely. Remember you are building and climbing a well-constructed staircase that's aimed at "living happily ever after" in a very real sense. But *you* have to make it work.

On the surface these steps seem naïvely simple. But most answers to life's problems are simple, like "start exercising," "stop smoking," "stop eating fatty foods," "start managing your stress," "stop letting it bother you." Simple is not necessarily *easy*. Do not let the surface simplicity mislead you into assuming that the journey can be accomplished without energy and courage. It takes courage to make any major change in your life. It takes courage to prepare for and enter into a permanent partnership. And you deserve to pat yourself on the back every time you move forward.

You may be thinking, "Why bother with this? Haven't I learned all I need to know from past experiences? The problem is to find someone and get married. I just don't want to be alone or lonely." Who hasn't experienced sitting home alone on a Saturday night feeling as if the rest of the world is made up of loving couples and yearning to be one of them? Or who hasn't experienced being lonely on a special holiday imagining everyone else having a warm, loving time—family tables spread with homemade goodies and fires crackling in the fireplaces. Yes, we can feel a desperate longing just to find someone. Anyone! When we think about committing ourselves to a partnership, it helps to realize the gravity of what we are signing up for.

Cynthia: Cynthia's story demonstrates how infantile an approach to partnership can be. At 17 she and her teenage boyfriend drove across the state line and got married. She recalls, "My boyfriend didn't have anything else to do that afternoon." She had hated her parents' arguing and bickering but was devastated by the thought of their getting a divorce. As her anger grew, all she could think of was to "get even with them." Getting married was her revenge. It was also the beginning of a sequence of four, failed marriages which resulted in two sons. Each time she felt tremendous attraction to her soon-to-be husband but the relationship didn't last. She remained totally unaware of her motivations until she entered therapy at the age of 48. There are thousands of Cynthias.

The five steps to permanent partnership are about changing your view of marriage, your view of yourself and your view of others. The magic in these steps is that they will not only enable you to find a permanent partner, but they also will enable you to practice the very skills you'll need to sustain that partnership. In Chapter 6, we will discuss more fully what it takes to sustain a permanent partnership. Only the gods know *all* the answers but we'll share what we've learned.

Focus on Yourself

First, you must focus on yourself. You must be in the right frame of mind to embark on this rewarding, but unknown, journey. Pilots say that landing a plane is easy if the approach is correct. If the plane is aligned properly, it practically lands itself. Finding the love of your life is like landing a plane. It happens almost automatically if you are adequately prepared, and if your approach is correct. The right preparation involves recognition and readiness. If deep down you are not ready for a real partnership, you may fail to act in your own best interests. As a result, it will be almost impossible to recognize your new partner even if this person arrives right on your doorstep.

Pamela: As adventure-loving Pamela put it, "If I had met Oliver five years earlier, the fact is I would not have gone for him because he is too nice. Oliver is a completely good person, truly a good man. He has no malice. He doesn't gossip. His is a good, sweet, lovely soul which shines in my eyes. Who he is has taught me how to love and how to trust. But if I had met him even one year earlier, I would have walked away from him. He wasn't dangerous enough and danger is what I'd looked for and hooked up with in the past—even when I got hurt along the way."

To recognize a person who is appropriate for you, you need to start acknowledging and dealing with any relationsickness you may have learned from past experiences. Relationsickness is discussed more fully in the next chapter. Understanding it will help you to make constructive decisions about where to start your journey toward permanent partnership. Dr. Victor Eisentein warned many years ago that being in love is not enough. "The transition from that strangely ambivalent obsession which we call 'being in love' to the capacity to really love another human being is one of the most important and difficult and intricate phenomena of human life . . ."[5]

Remember, if you have experienced a failed relationship that does not make you a failure. Modern marriage is not easy. It is a wonderful challenge and responsibility for which most of us are little or ill-prepared. However, with time and effort well spent, a satisfying marriage can certainly be in your future. Somewhere there is a person who is an appropriate permanent partner for you. Follow the Matching Process and you will have a better-than-average chance of finding fulfillment. You *can* create a love that lasts.

About the Questions and Exercises

At the end of each chapter, you will find Questions and Exercises which we designed to provoke your memories, your beliefs, your attitudes and to give you insights, ideas and clarity. They have grown out of our experience as counselors, teachers and trainers. You can certainly gain from this book even without doing them. However, they will help you personalize and apply the information discussed in each chapter. We suggest that you read through them first and then select for completion those questions and exercises that seem the most relative to you and your unique experiences. The exercises take thought and time but they help to tell you about yourself and raise your awareness.

The book is organized so that you can write your responses in it. If writing in your book does not appeal to you, we suggest that you keep a separate journal. As you read each chapter, make notes of those things that are meaningful to you, notes that you can add to later, review and study.

As you move along in the materials, we recommend that you make contracts with yourself about steps you actually intend to take and how and when you intend to take them. Contracts force clarity and make it easier for you to know when you are making headway toward changes you desire. You will find a sample contract in Appendix B.

Questions and Exercises

Memories and Programming: We designed the following questions to trigger some of the memories and programming that impact your current attitudes and beliefs. What you learn to believe about yourself, about marriage and about life in general will shape both your feelings and your behavior.

Think about and jot down the attitudes and beliefs you have learned about marriage.

1. Were you encouraged to "fall in love" as the first step to marriage?
   a) Whose "voice" is telling you what is a proper path?

   b) What are your current feelings about this?

2. What roles did you learn men should assume?
   a) In courtship?

   b) In marriage?

   c) In life?

3. What roles did you learn women should assume?
   a) In courtship?

   b) In marriage?

   c) In life?

4. What expectations did you learn to have? What was marriage to be like?

5. What attitudes were you taught about divorce?

6. How do these attitudes affect you now?

In regard to the seven clues mentioned earlier that help you assess how a relationship is progressing, have you had any personal, first-hand experiences with any of these issues in a past or current relationship?

1. The way you were treated as a person.

2. How soon physical involvement developed and the consequences.

3. How the relationship grew.

4. Reciprocity.

5. Best friends.

6. Communication patterns.

7. Enhanced well-being, accepted for yourself.

If so, what did you learn from these encounters?

Start thinking about what permanent partnership might mean to you. What is it you want in order to be happy in a long-term relationship?

What sex roles (expectations of men and women determined on the basis of their sex), if any, do you see as important to permanent partnership?

What are your expectations of marriage in one year?

10 years?

20 years?

30 years?

40 or more years?

How do you envision growing old together?

Do you see things about yourself right now that you may need to work on in order to be a successful permanent partner in a long-term relationship?

If so, what are they?

ENDNOTES

1. See Robert O. Blood, Jr., *Love Match and Arranged Marriage*, The Free Press, 1967, pp. 4–6.

2. M. Scott Peck, *The Road Less Traveled*, Simon & Schuster, 1978, p. 92.

3. For more information regarding family violence, battered women and their families, contact: Battered Women's Alternatives, P.O. Box 6406, Concord, CA 94524. Also, contact the National Organization for Women, 1000 16th Street N. W., Suite 700, Washington, D.C. 20036. The National Victims Center's INFOLINK program provides a comprehensive, toll-free source of information on over 60 crime and victim-related subjects as well as referral to thousands of service providers across the nation. Call 1-800-FYI-CALL.

4. Kahlil Gibran, *The Prophet*, Alfred A. Knopf, New York, 1966, p. 16.

5. Victor W. Eisentein, M.D., *Neurotic Interaction in Marriage*, Basic Books, New York, 1956, p. 31 (from a section contributed by Lawrence S. Kukie, M.D., "Psychoanalysis and Marriage, Practical and Theoretical Issues").

Chapter 2

Step 1: Part 1
Recognizing Relationsickness

❤————————————————————❤

We have met the enemy and he is us.
Walt Kelley

Have you ever plunged head long into a relationship knowing it was doomed? Have you ever found yourself attracted to someone you knew deep in your heart wasn't good for you? Are you in a relationship now that makes you unhappy but feel you just can't leave? Do you avoid relationships for fear of being hurt? Do you feel that either men or women can't be trusted?

While almost everyone has experienced at least some discomfort with relationships, many of us have experienced a great deal of pain and discomfort, some of it repetitive. Such pain and discomfort are the main symptoms of "relationsickness." This chapter is to help you recognize and acknowledge any relationsickness that might be standing in your way. The next chapter is about selecting an appropriate cure.

Transcending relationsickness is the first and most potent measure you can take toward finding a love that lasts. We become relationsick when we distort our perception of ourselves in ways that result in low self-esteem, self-contempt or grandiosity—thinking that we are worse or better than other people. It is also affected by whatever we learn to think and feel about others—especially unrealistic or unusual expectations. These perceptions and opinions affect how we think, feel and relate to a potential partner. If you really think about it, perception means everything and it's entirely in our minds. An emotion is a bodily response to a thought. What we've learned to think triggers our emotions, which, in turn, provides the energy for what we choose to do.

You have seen relationsickness. One way it manifests itself is in feeling attracted to others who simply aren't good for us. The forms it takes range from the mild, "I just can't seem to communicate with that woman," to the tragic and traumatic, "I know he beats me but I love him and can't leave." It can also be experienced by feeling lukewarm toward a wonderfully appropriate man or woman.

Many Causes

Relationsickness has many causes some of which we do not understand at all. They just seem to be there. Certainly being brought up in a stable, loving, functional family is the very best way to know how to create such a family yourself. However, some people who have been brought up in such families still have trouble establishing a healthy, long-lasting relationship with a partner. Some causes may always elude us but many causes we do understand. We know, for example, if a little girl's father brutalizes her, she makes a decision deep in her soul that "men are no good and will only try to hurt me." She also may be confused. The one man she wants most to love—and to be loved and protected by—relates to her with cruelty and unbridled emotions. She may not understand why, but until she resolves these old feelings and until she makes new decisions, she will be attracted to men who abuse her, or to milk-sops who fear life and never raise their voices. If a little boy is belittled, brutalized, seduced, abandoned or overprotected by his mother, he may make negative decisions about women that are later reinforced by negative relationships. It is estimated that one out of three girls and one out of seven boys are molested before age 18. Most experts agree that incidences reported are just the tip of the iceberg. This seems especially true for boys. As a result, tens of millions of adults have had their capacity for intimacy severely impaired.[1]

Yes, we create our view of the world in childhood and then try to keep that world in place. If we become relationsick, rather than look for better qualities in a potential mate, we tend to look either for the same traits—subtle or blatant—we grew up knowing (how we believe things are to be), or we look for the extreme opposites. For example, it is well known that abusive parents usually have abusive parents themselves. Some abusive behavior in families can be traced for well over 100 years (which is why it can be useless to blame our parents for our problems). Children from dysfunctional families find kindness hard to trust. In turn, they are unable to express kindness or to develop trust in their own children. On and on the cycle goes. This is how we create our own realities. Perception is the key. The world is the way we see it.

Life as Teacher

Life has a way of saying to us, "Until you outgrow the blueprints of old experiences and distorted beliefs about yourself and others, you will keep being attracted to people who reinforce these beliefs." This phenomenon results in our subconsciously choosing people who are "wrong" for our present happiness, but "right" in terms of representing unresolved and unfinished business from the past. When we are attracted to someone for this reason, it may well bring out the worst in us. But, with proper guidance and insight, it can provide opportunities to learn about ourselves—our deepest feelings, our shame, our guilt, our anger, lust, sadness, fears, low self-worth—whatever thoughts and subsequent feelings we have stored in our memory banks. In a sense, these people can become our "teachers" and give us lessons about unfinished business from the past. Unfortunately, learning through life's lessons is time-consuming, painful and often difficult to do without help. This book can help you carefully analyze some of the dynamics of what has happened to you. It can point you in a new direction and help you decide on a new path rather than blaming yourself and others for failed relationships. Here are two stories that illustrate how others are often mirrors to ourselves.

Muriel: Muriel, a bright, conscientious specialist in data-processing, explains how Life as teacher worked for her: "My failed relationship with Bret taught me two great lessons. You see, my friends were shocked when they met him. I had been telling them about this wonderful, kind, handsome man I had met who was everything I ever wanted in a mate. They all saw somebody very different from the person I described and couldn't understand why I was so attracted to him. It wasn't until the relationship was over that I really thought about what had happened. Then through talking with close friends, seeing a psychotherapist, and keeping a journal of my feelings, I finally realized the truth. Bret was wonderful and kind only to his daughter whom he saw twice a year when she came to visit. He certainly wasn't any of those things to me, in fact he was quite the opposite: never faithful, honest or nurturing. But, even so, I remained addicted to him because I had always wanted a father like him instead of the father I have. I kept seeing Bret as the father to his daughter, instead of facing the reality of Bret as he related to me. What a lesson that was! The funny thing is, when it was all over, I also realized why my friends were so dumbfounded about my insistence on how good-looking he was. In reality he did not present a stereotypical 'handsome' picture. He was short, very overweight, bald, and always smoking a smelly cigar. He bore a remarkable resemblance to my grandfather, the only man from my childhood who had been nice to me, but who under no circumstances would be considered handsome. Love is blind in more ways than one. But I did finally learn. I learned to see a man for who he actually was, not who I wanted him to be."

Muriel's experience seems almost bizarre to anyone who hasn't experienced such distortions of perception. Happily her vision eventually cleared up. Bret "helped" her to do this.

Rob: Rob had a similar revelation after he analyzed why he had been so enthralled with Rebecca even though she had caused him much more sadness than happiness. "I realize now that Rebecca was the perfect person for me—not perfect in the sense of being the right mate but perfect for me to confront the issues of my childhood. I just didn't know how to deal with them in a healthy way. Rebecca always kept me guessing. I never could depend on her to keep a date, remember my birthday or comfort me when I needed it. In fact, she informed me she wanted more freedom right after I told her I had lost my biggest account at work. Even though her actions hurt a lot, I found the relationship 'exciting.' Every time I broke it off, I would come running back at the first hint that she wanted me to. I was taking two graduate courses in the psychology of personality and, with some soul searching, eventually came to realize that my attraction to Rebecca was to a large part based on my experience with my older sister whom I adored but who treated me with devastating indifference. She died when she was 22 and I never fully resolved whether or not she really loved me. I was using Rebecca to figure this out. It seems pretty silly now that I realize what was going on, but it was very powerful at the time."

Transcending Relationsickness

Hopefully, we will transcend relationsickness when we:

- ♥ recognize and admit to any distortions or hurts from the past;
- ♥ work on getting these resolved;
- ♥ put these defeating parts of our pasts where they belong—behind us;
- ♥ and get on with who we *really* can be.

Life is rarely perfect but it *can* be a lot happier. And growth takes us to a whole new level of possibilities and experiences.

Yes, relationsickness has many roots and affects us in many ways. Here are a few examples from clinical practice. Do any of these cases ring a bell with you?

Fred: Fred tells about his relationship with his mother. She neither beat him nor abused him physically in any way, but she constantly reminded him of his inadequacies. No matter what he did or how hard he tried, it was never right nor good enough nor clever enough. She chided him that he wasn't tall enough nor handsome enough either. Years of verbal castigation finally brought him to the decision: "I'm no good, I can't do anything right!" To reinforce his beliefs about himself, Fred learned to provoke even his teachers to put him down. His first wife described her frustrations, "I know I'm on his case all the time but he just drives me up the wall." Fred began to understand that he was attracted to women who would indeed "get on his case." And, for his part, he knew how to make it happen. Very big leaps in self-worth and self-confidence were important steps in his recovery. He then had no need to seek put-downs from women in order to maintain his childlike image of himself and his world. However, not all profound influences occur in childhood.

Paul: Paul had a happy and supportive childhood and turned into an exceptional real estate salesperson. In his early 20's, he was riding high and encouraging friends to ride with him through buying properties. When a recession hit, the dreams came tumbling down. Paul fell into a deep financial hole and experienced traumatic anxiety and depression over his friends' losses which he couldn't correct. "I've hurt the people I love the most." This precipitous loss of self-esteem and ensuing hopelessness caused Paul to fear and avoid relationships. His ability to attract women who were confident, educated and had high self-esteem was greatly diminished until he regained his own self-esteem and turned his full energy in a new direction.

The previous cases were rather dramatic and even traumatic, but relationsickness can grow out of far more subtle circumstances. It was what *didn't* happen to John that seemed to affect him the most.

John: John had no significant male figure in his life as he grew up. His mother was a hard-working, conscientious woman who treated him well and did her best to bring up "her little man." John, however, felt isolated and frustrated. He was unsure of himself as a budding man and, as a teenager, was picked up several times by the police for petty theft and defacing property. "I knew what I was doing was wrong, but somehow it made me feel big. I really thought I had to be a tough guy to be a real man." He later took to car racing in order to prove his manliness. His compulsion to prove himself was one way of coping with trying to grow up male when he had no one who cared about him to show him how. Later, John was attracted to women who were motherly toward him. He had great difficulty establishing an egalitarian relationship and felt quite unsure about his masculinity. Joining a men's support group and establishing a "fatherly" relationship with an older man were key factors in his healing and recovery from relationsickness.

Janet: Janet also experienced no harsh treatment. She described herself as "adored by my father." He called her his sweet little doll, dressed her in fancy clothes, intervened to smooth out any frustrations that came her way, was unhappy if she became boisterous or dirty, and eventually wanted her to go to finishing school, but not to college. She felt guilty if she rebelled against his wishes because he "loved" her so much. Janet had almost no personal resourcefulness as an adult yet described herself as "better than most people." She found herself attracted to men who wanted to take care of her. However, she would soon grow bored and move on to a "more exciting" man, but always to one who wanted her to remain his little girl. A willingness to grow up and take risks and personal responsibilities were critical to her recovery.

Linda: On the surface it appeared as if Linda's parents were happily married. They rarely fought and maintained an image of tranquility. In reality, however, the surface calm hid an ocean of discontent. They secretly blamed this situation on having married when they were still teenagers. They repeatedly warned Linda, "Don't get married young." What Linda heard and internalized was, "Don't get married." She avoided men, would only date the same one a few times, and always had a plausible excuse for not being involved in a relationship. It wasn't until she found herself single and in her mid 30's that she explored these early messages. This exploration made her realize how her "programming" had impacted the choices she was making about men and marriage.

Eric: Eric remembers his father as cool and aloof. "He was like a phantom who appeared and disappeared and I never knew for sure who was behind his mask. In school I was described as shy and withdrawn. The only pal I remember called me Mystery Man. Girls scared me to death. I could never seem to relate to women the way other guys did. Later, when I finally made friends with a woman, I panicked when we started to get close. The only man I knew how to be like was my father. It feels like a big void, a dark scary place that if I try to enter, I freeze."

It took many years for Eric to overcome his relationsickness. Keys to his recovery were a willingness to take risks, understanding and expressing his feelings, developing close friendships with older men, and being vulnerable in relationships. His steps were gradual and deliberate.

All of these individuals suffered from some degree of relationsickness. Although they may not have recognized that deep-seated decisions about themselves affected their capacities to love and be loved, at some level they knew that their relationships were not going well. Subconscious decisions affect us in many ways. At an early age, many of us develop fairy tale, mythological or storybook beliefs about ourselves. At a deep level they can form our expected life stories and compel us to seek certain people to play the roles that perpetuate our own. These people must fulfill our expectations and "help" us act out our predetermined dramas—our life scripts.[2] For example, in order to play a victim role in life such as Sleeping Beauty or the Little Lame Prince, someone else must play the persecutor or the rescuer. Our personal mythology can push us realistically, but it also can be twisted, unrealistic and compel us to fill our lives with unhappiness. The patterns and compulsions that drive us from within need to be examined.

Fairy Tales and Myths

Inside us lurk heroes, heroines, villains, kings, queens, warriors, peasants, priestesses, adventurers, magicians, fools, dictators, lovers, martyrs, healers, and so forth. We can have many characters—sub-personalities—residing in us who compel us to play certain roles, seek out certain people to play the complementary parts, and fulfill certain compelling dramas. Depending on our actual experiences, these parts might be acted out in a positive way bringing us happiness and fulfillment and giving our life direction and purpose. Or, they can be acted out in a negative way manifesting our dark or shadow side. For example, we can be real fairy godmothers or fairy godfathers who give someone else an opportunity of a lifetime with no strings attached. Or, we can be play-acting and phony with our rescuing—perhaps unable to deliver what was promised or fouling things up and then pleading, "I was only trying to help you." We can be warriors whose willingness to fight for what's right is governed by an inner priest or noble royalty. Or, we can be warriors who strike out with violence, without conscience, void of any higher governing principles.

You might recognize one or more of the following characters in your life:

Atlas who insists on carrying the burden of the world on his shoulders. (Yes, there are Lady Atlases, too.)

Cinderella (or Cinderfella) who plays the waiting game yearning to be rescued by someone else from a cruel and menial life.

The potential Prince who has suffered a wicked spell that turned him into a frog, living well below his potential possibilities while waiting to be rescued and loved.

Hera, wife of the god Zeus, who, overcome with jealousy, endlessly stalks after her womanizing husband.

Peter Pan who never wants to grow up and who looks for a younger woman to help keep him that way.

The Tough Woman who impregnably shields her body so that no one can reach her tender feelings.

The Knight in Shining Armor who rescues damsels in distress and then abandons them to search for the next dragon because he is more happy in dangerous situations than loving ones.

Medusa who, cursed for adulterous wrong-doing, turns others to stone with her looks, warding off all who pursue her.

Watan a dominant god who strips his favorite daughter Brunhilda of her godlike powers and banishes her to a deep sleep on a fiery mountain because she dared to disobey him.

Little Mermaid who is willing to give up her home, culture, family and even her body in order to win the affection of a man whom she has only glimpsed and never spoken to.

Prince Eric, the object of Little Mermaid's affections, who decides to marry her, even though all he remembers about her is her voice. (As a consequence, he agrees to marry a disguised witch who has captured that voice.)

Or we can be Beauty who seeks one Beast after another, only to find that her magic fails to turn any of her Beasts into the handsome Prince she hoped for. (It is not uncommon for the model of her Beast to have been an addicted parent who was ugly to her yet whom she felt compelled to rescue.)

Clearly our experiences and decisions give us a powerful imprint—a system of beliefs, thoughts, feelings, roles and opinions that stick. When negative, such experiences make dire contributions to relationsickness. They shape "instincts" which then mislead us. Consequently, we fail to act in our own best interests. Rather than being attracted to real potential permanent partners, to the prince or princess we deserve, bells ring and chemistry sizzles for the wrong people.

High quality, potential mates can seem invisible, or unrecognizable or disguised. We don't seem to see them for their goodness and appropriateness. They may be disguised in bodies that don't seem right, have the wrong personality type, be in the wrong occupation, drive the wrong kind of car or be "too nice" and not exciting enough. Whatever the so-called problem with the other person, *relationsick people usually are not attracted to people capable of permanent partnerships.* Deep down they are not ready for a committed, intimate, accepting, enduring relationship. They let themselves be guided by negative standards or superficial qualities such as appearance, status or material possessions. It is not that these traits have no importance, but if they are your only "turn-on" and you "turn-off" to high quality people, you will never find the love of your life. This nearly happened to Lauren, one of the women we interviewed.

Lauren and Ralph: Lauren is intelligent, educated and sparkles with energy. She had known Ralph for 15 years before she fell in love with him. They had been best friends for all of this time. Ralph wanted more, but Lauren kept finding herself attracted to men who had "the souls of artists." She followed an unpublished novelist to the desert and supported them both by waitressing even though she had a degree in biology and suitable job prospects in the little town in which the novelist wanted to live. When he pulled up stakes and left her broke and pregnant, it was Ralph's shoulder she cried on. It was Ralph who helped her through her ordeal. After her failed marriage to a pianist, Ralph was the one who offered her a place to stay to recuperate. Ralph was the friend who listened, who was first to help, and who could always be depended on to be there when needed. He saw something in Lauren that she didn't see herself. It wasn't until Lauren faced her situation and behavior that she could transcend relationsickness. She finally realized what a wonderful person Ralph was and the many ways he was attractive: intellectually, emotionally and physically. Her relationsickness had caused her to make irresponsible decisions about the role of a man in her life and had prevented her from recognizing a perfect permanent partner— Ralph, her best friend for almost half of her life.

See what you can learn from the following questionnaire. The questions are based on the behaviors that people exhibited who had to heal their capacity for intimacy, trust and commitment. Careful consideration can help you clarify those behaviors which you might manifest and to what degree you are relationsick. Think of each question on a scale of 1 to 5, with 1 meaning that you agree that you always do this and 5 being the other extreme—you disagree and never do this. Circle the number that best describes you.

Relationsick Questionnaire

1. I am mainly attracted to people who are bad for me.   *1 2 3 4 5*

2. When I meet an eligible person, I start thinking our future will end unhappily.   *1 2 3 4 5*

3. I find it easy to have friends of the opposite sex, but I can't fall in love.   *1 2 3 4 5*

4. If someone really knew me, they wouldn't like me.   *1 2 3 4 5*

5. I find that I embellish facts about myself when I meet someone new.   *1 2 3 4 5*

6. I have very few friends of the opposite sex.   *1 2 3 4 5*

7. I know I won't meet anybody nice, so I just don't bother going out.   *1 2 3 4 5*

8. It's not a big problem to meet new people, but after the first few dates it falls apart.   *1 2 3 4 5*

9. When I start dating someone, things are wonderful until we have sex.   *1 2 3 4 5*

10. When I start dating someone, things are wonderful until I really start liking the person.   *1 2 3 4 5*

11. The only people who seem to like me are those whom I don't like.   *1 2 3 4 5*

12. I can't relax and be "me" when I meet someone eligible.   *1 2 3 4 5*

13. I believe that all the nice men/women are already taken.   *1 2 3 4 5*

14. There's only one right way to meet someone.   *1 2 3 4 5*

15. I wish that arranged marriages were still the norm.   *1 2 3 4 5*

16. I don't want anyone to know I'm ready to settle down.   *1 2 3 4 5*

17. I'll give up the unsatisfying relationship I'm in now once I meet someone better.   *1 2 3 4 5*

18. The person I'm involved with now can't marry me, but some day this will change.   *1 2 3 4 5*

19. My relationships seem to have patterns to them, even when I think I'm changing.   *1 2 3 4 5*

20. The men/women I trust seem to be nice in the beginning, but then turn out to be wrong for me.   *1 2 3 4 5*

21. I find it hard to trust someone of the opposite sex. *1 2 3 4 5*

22. I don't like someone once that person likes me. *1 2 3 4 5*

23. I can't help it, my type just isn't the marrying kind. *1 2 3 4 5*

24. I am mainly attracted to a perfect body type (or occupation or talent). *1 2 3 4 5*

25. I'm turned off by someone who seems appropriate for me. *1 2 3 4 5*

26. I can't tell if a person is appropriate for me. *1 2 3 4 5*

27. When I meet someone who appears to be a quality person, usually I'm wrong. *1 2 3 4 5*

28. If my looks were different, it would be no problem finding a mate. *1 2 3 4 5*

29. If I had a different job (lived in a better neighborhood, drove a different car, had better clothes), I could find a mate. *1 2 3 4 5*

30. Nice men/women are boring. *1 2 3 4 5*

You can tell that there is really no definitive way to score the above quiz. However, you can certainly use it as a guide. For example, if you look back at your number of 4's and 5's and see that you have 20 or so, you probably do not suffer from relationsickness. In that case, the next three chapters may not be useful to you and you may want to proceed directly to the procedures on how to meet people of integrity, Chapter 7, "Take Charge." Be grateful that you have learned self-supporting attitudes and beliefs about yourself and about possible mates. Thank the people and influences in your life that helped you accomplish this because you do not have to hit rock bottom and do the necessary healing to be ready for a partnership.

On the other hand, if you marked 10 or more 1's and 2's, read on. You probably have some degree of relationsickness and will need to take the steps to recovery one at a time. Relationsickness is curable. Don't let the news that you have some work to do discourage you. Don't think you can't have it all and will have to compromise yourself if you want a partnership. It may seem strange, but in almost every one of our cases, the people who followed the five-step Matching Process experienced their partners to be more than they dared hope for—more caring, nurturing, thoughtful; more stimulating and dynamic and many even more economically sound. Does anyone ever experience finding a new and permanent mate an easy task? The answer is "Yes!"

However, the majority of those interviewed, although wanting very much to find mates, fell into one failed relationship after another. They experienced relationsickness by being unhappy, feeling incomplete, feeling inadequate, feeling life was unfair, feeling depressed, feeling hurt, and being dissatisfied much of the time. What fascinated us was that this very diverse group eventually did learn the secrets of finding the right partner. Although it certainly wasn't easy and they had many painful experiences, they somehow found their way to the same sequence of steps used by the others which eventually led them all to permanent partners. But first they had to change *the way they thought about finding their mates.* These thoughts which were mentioned in the introduction made a big difference:

- ❤ meeting potential partners is relatively easy;
- ❤ being a permanent partner is very challenging;
- ❤ the path to being one does not require external changes;
- ❤ but internal changes which lead to liking oneself more are essential.

Accepting these four basic concepts and then acting upon them was the magic used by relationsick people to start healing and empowering themselves to become permanent partners. While these concepts involve all of the steps of the Matching Process, accepting that they had to make internal changes was a core motivator and an essential part of the first step, "Heal Any Wounds." Changing their thinking was necessary and put them well on their way to making the Matching Process work for them.

The good news is that relationsickness is curable. You do not have to discover the cure through trial and error all by yourself. While it is true that growing pains can hurt, in the long run, having the courage to face up to who and what you've been—to acknowledge that you have a dark side—that you've made inappropriate choices, provokes you to grow. You may have heard the saying, "Out of the mud grows a lotus." Our own "murky" experiences, no matter how painful, most always contain gems of learning. Growth, a heightened consciousness and maturity lead to better choices and decisions. Indeed, there is hope. Remember *all of the people* we interviewed who had had troubled relationships took the steps in the Matching Process and found their way to permanent partnership. So take heart! It can happen to you.

Questions and Exercises

Each of us acts out the problems of negative programming in our own way. If you are trying to become aware of your choices, see what insights you gain from the following questions and exercises. If you suffer from some degree of relationsickness, you either have a set of unrealistic or superficial standards for yourself and for potential partners or you are attracted to those who will make your life painful . . . or both.

Your Relationship Patterns: What attracts you now in a potential partner? Write down the traits of which you are conscious (both positive and negative) as you think about those with whom you have been involved. Be as honest and as accurate as you can possibly be.

Could any of the traits you mentioned be considered superficial or unrealistic? Are you tempted to focus on externals such as appearance (i.e., tall, dark, and handsome, or cute, little blond)? Write down any self discoveries.

Look at what you've written in response to the two previous questions. Go deeper. Be extremely honest with yourself and think hard about your past partners. Take a really close look at what turns you on and draws you to a person—good and bad. What actually happened in your last relationship? What roles did you play: victim, rescuer, persecutor? What patterns do you see? Think not only about traits but also about behaviors. What did you and your partner do? How did you treat each other? Make this description as complete as you possibly can because it holds a key to any relationsickness you might be harboring.

Now study what you have written above:

Do your descriptions remind you of anyone from your past?

If so, is this a positive or a negative? A mixture?

In what kind of patterns (repeated actions and roles) do you see yourself involved?

As a child, did you have a favorite storybook, TV, fairy tale, or mythological character?

How did this character relate to the opposite sex?

Do you see this character being played out in your relationships in any way?

How realistic are your expectations? Are you envisioning a fantasy, an idealized type of relationship, or can you see yourself functioning in a day-in-day-out kind of life with its ups and downs and growth problems?

Would your expectations (above) suit you for a long-term relationship, or are they childlike and immature or in any way wrong for you? Can you see how they could be more realistic?

Looking at the possibility that you modeled yourself after your same-sexed parent figure, think about:

What decisions did I make about myself as a result of interactions with this parent figure?

What sex-roles were expected?

What was expected in a relationship such as marriage?

What did I see this person doing that I'm doing now?

What did I learn about being a man or a woman from this person?

What have I learned about myself from this exploration that will help me be part of a successful, permanent partnership?

Looking at the possibility that you think and feel about the opposite sex in many ways similar to the ways you thought and felt about your opposite-sexed parent figure (father, mother, uncle, aunt, grandfather, grandmother—whoever was there), describe:

What decisions did I make about myself as a result of interactions with this parent figure?

What specific decisions did I make about my sexuality?

What sex-roles did I learn to expect from this parent figure?

How did I learn to treat the opposite sex from this person?

What opinions and expectations did I learn to have about the opposite sex?

Which of these influences were positive for me and which were negative?

What men or women have I felt attracted to in my life who are like this person (or just the opposite)?

What patterns of interaction were repeated?

How did these relationships work for me?

What have I learned about myself from this exploration that will help me be part of a successful, permanent relationship?

With your answers to these questions in mind, think about how realistic or unrealistic your beliefs about yourself are. Sort these out and write them down.

Realistic:

Unrealistic:

Think about any traumatic experience you have had:
What feelings and opinions have stuck with you as a result of this trauma?

How has this affected your self-respect and your caring for and about yourself?

Crystallize for yourself any traits you are attracted to that, in the long run, are *bad* for you. Write them down.

Now crystallize any *good* decisions you have made about relationships and write them down.

How do the "bad" and "good" balance out?

What are specific traits you are ready to look for *now* in a permanent partner?

ENDNOTES

1. For obvious reasons, accurate statistics concerning child molestation are difficult to obtain. Here are a few references to give you a guide. See D. Finkelhor, *Child Sexual Abuse: New Theories and Research*, New York: Free Press, 1984. Sandra Butler, *Conspiracy of Silence*, New Glide Publication, San Francisco, 1978. Diana Russell, *The Secret Trauma*, Basic Books, New York, 1986. Contact the National Committee for the Prevention of Child Abuse, 332 South Michigan Avenue #1250, Chicago, IL 60604; the U.S. Attorney General, Washington, D.C., the Child Assault Prevention Training Center of California, 51 Jack London Square, Oakland, CA 94607, or Child Abuse Prevention Council of Contra Costa County, 1485 Treat Blvd., Suite 202, Walnut Creek, CA 94596. See full transcript of "Phil Donahue Show," March 15, 1991, Show #0315-91, Transcript #3163, Donahue Transcripts, 267 Broadway, New York, NY, 10007 with Johanna Gallers, Ph.D., former Director of the Valley Trauma Center in Northridge, CA.

2. For more information about life scripts, see Muriel James and Dorothy Jongeward, *Born to Win*, and Dorothy Jongeward and Dru Scott, *Women as Winners*, both Addison-Wesley Publishing, Reading, MA. Also, see Moore and Gillette, *King, Warrior, Magician, and Lover*, Harper, San Francisco, 1990.

Chapter 3

Step 1: Part 2
Heal Any Wounds

❤━━━━━━━━━━━━━━━━━━━━━━━━━━━━━━━━━━━━━━━❤

Mythology tells us that where you stumble, that's where your treasure is.
Joseph Campbell

If you have experienced an unhappy, failed or hostile relationship in the past, you know that it can be a devastating experience. Our psyches can be left feeling traumatized, beaten and exhausted. Fears can give us pangs of anguish and uncertainty. Can I trust getting close? Will I be hurt? Am I attractive? Who would love me if they really knew me? Can I handle the dating game? Am I going to be rejected? There are bound to be wounds—some of them open and sore and deep. Time may heal many of them but others may need a little help. Regaining confidence and self-esteem can take time, energy and even money. But what could you invest in better than yourself and your future happiness?

There's little question that this effort requires *making significant internal changes.* The focus here is on getting you ready for permanent partnership by shedding some light on persistent patterns, changing your perception—the way you see the world and yourself in it, and opening up new choices. Emotions left over from old, unhappy relationships need to be resolved and released. If not, we have a high tendency to keep repeating ourselves. A misprogrammed, subconscious mind wields a great deal of influence and needs to be reprogrammed. If you are carrying with you any degree of relationsickness for whatever reason, the most wonderful potential partner could be right under your very nose and you wouldn't know it. To change this unhappy circumstance, you must heal your hurts in order to ready yourself for positive change and new beginnings.

The Intention to Heal

What most of the people we interviewed needed to do to get the Matching Process working for them was to commit to healing. This, in turn, created a readiness for new perspectives that transcended old patterns. There is little question that the intensity of our desire affects our level of willingness to invest the time and energy it takes to ready ourselves for lasting relationships. Without that strong intent, most of us will end up being repeaters. The strength garnered from intention can give you the push to take that first step. The intention holds its own magic.

Giving Up Relationsickness

Giving up old patterns isn't always easy, but it almost always means that something new is in the offing. Step One implies a readiness to greet the new. It can mean being ready to *get* something—something different. Perhaps it's a relationship that supports your health and well-being. Perhaps it's a spiritual partner. Perhaps it's a home and a family. Perhaps it's a companion and a mother or father for your children. But it can also mean being ready to *give up* something—to let something go. Here's how Marianne, a well-educated, methodical and deliberate woman in her early 40's, expressed her shift in perception when she gave up holding on to the past.

Marianne: "My first marriage was made with the best of intentions to a well-established psychiatrist on the East Coast who was 11 years older than I. He seemed to offer everything that I wanted—intelligence, position, security—but was very, very needy. I'm a rescuer by nature and here was this needy, emotional man. On the surface he appeared to be 'together.' We seemed to come from the same kind of life, want the same kind of life, but I just didn't read it accurately. If I had to say why I picked my second husband, I don't think I picked him for different reasons at all. But I do think I was *far more accurate in what I perceived in him as a person.*

"I was raised in a lifestyle where I was trained to be an accommodator. I was the sweetest, most wonderful wife and trained to be that way—trained to so bury my own needs that I didn't even know how to identify them. But I was also trained to believe that my rewards would come from being this really good, kind, wonderful person. One of my most graphic images of myself is walking one of my kids in the park and holding up my head to the heavens and saying, 'So, where's my reward?' When I opened my mouth to speak, bird shit fell in! And that personified exactly what was happening in my marriage.

"My first husband was an anxiety-ridden man when I met him and he was worse when I left. He wasn't even kind to me. By the middle of our marriage, it was very clear I no longer loved him. But I had a two-year-old and a newborn. I also had a stepchild that I was raising. So I made a deal with myself to stay until I felt I could leave.

"For five years from the point when I knew I was going to do it, I used to console myself at night when I was most miserable. Like a kid hugs a teddy-bear, I would console myself with my timetable. I'd run it through my mind and remind myself that I was not going to be here forever, that I was not locked in.

"Yes, I didn't leave for five long years. But when I made that decision, I stopped being angry. I stopped feeling bitter. I knew why I was there. And I will always remember my face going from intense tightness to 'it didn't matter anymore what he was.' I didn't ask anything more of him. I didn't require anything of him. It was difficult, but it was easier than always feeling deprived and disappointed. I think that's when the healing started.

"There was no question when I was actually ready to leave. I remember, though, what kept me from doing it earlier. I called it, 'the dinner-party syndrome,' where you look on your calendar and you say, 'Gee, I can't leave him this week. You know, we have this party coming up.' I did that kind of kidding around. But the fact is, you have to be ready enough so that nothing else matters. And when you're ready, you leave. So, when the right time came five years later, I just picked up and I left.

"My life had been so full of things, of material things. You have to not only be ready to leave the person, you have to be ready to leave your lifestyle. Things have to be bad enough or your survival important enough so that you can leave a lifestyle—because I left everything. Not only my friends, but everything. I was never able to collect things again. I live in a nice house now, but it's functional. It is not filled with the pretty things I loved collecting. I just couldn't do it again. I didn't have the energy any more. The losses can be so painful. I get a lump in my throat even talking about it."

Marianne knew for five years that she had to leave a very bad marriage. She had made a decision in her own behalf. Before she could actually walk out the door, she had to gain enough personal insight and start her path to healing in order to deal with her losses. She had to heal enough wounds to be ready to leave a comfortable lifestyle. She had to give up financial security. She had to give up her learned need to rescue. She had to give up a father for her children. She had to give up a prestigious place in the community. Healing for Marianne meant letting go of many things and gathering up the courage to face many unknowns. To let relationsickness go means something different for each person, but the process must get under way for the next steps to work.

Three Doses of Cures

The cure to giving up relationsickness comes in three dosages, each stronger than the last. The dose you should take depends on the seriousness of your condition and the level of discipline you are able to muster in your own behalf. The strength of the prescription should vary according to need. No particular cure is "better" than the other, but one will be the most appropriate for you. The important thing to remember is that they all lead to recovery, no matter which prescription for relationhealth you choose. While this may be a painful event, be excited that you are on your way to something fresh, something new. After all, if you are choosing not to live by a pre-determined script, a fairy-tale scenario which has produced a "bad show" for you, you might as well take control by writing the new script yourself. Why not create your own life story? Why not include as much happiness in the action and dialogue of your life drama as possible?

Small-Dose Cure

Pamela: Pamela, an energetic woman with a bit of a wild streak, was caught in what she thought was an adventurous, stimulating life. She had lived in many interesting places, collected exotic experiences, and dated a wide range of men. Although she told herself that she wanted to settle down, she didn't want to give up the casual and varied relationships which seemed, at least at the beginning, to be so exciting. Pamela didn't really care if the men she dated were married or single, emotionally available or not. What counted was their ability to sweep her up into their lifestyle. She enjoyed being a part of different lives at different times. Even though each time she got involved with a new man who showed her a different slice of life she would feel, "this is it; he's the one for me," the feeling was always temporary. Sooner or later, Pamela would get bored and move on. She described herself as having at least seven "emotional divorces."

One night, Pamela had a particularly distressing dream. She woke up with the stark realization that she would probably never fall in love permanently and get married. The thought terrified and shocked her. The message of this dream stayed with her for days. It was so powerful it caused a shift in her thinking. This change happened spontaneously and without conscious exertion on her part. Just realizing that the old ways would never give her the permanent partner she wanted was enough. The first overt sign that something was different was when Pamela's old "turn-ons" suddenly stopped being attractive. She had a whole different view of the life she was leading. She began to experience that a man's status, his exotic lifestyle, hobbies or possessions, weren't exciting any more. She ceased being dazzled by brilliance, special talent or unique ability. At first she found this change very uncomfortable and a little frightening. If the old turn-ons weren't there, what would make life exciting? In time, however, she became more in tune with men who were appropriate for her and her life goals. She found herself drawn to men because of who they were as human beings rather than their accomplishments, possessions or glitz.

When asked what had provoked the shift, Pamela answered, "What caused the change? That dream really stirred up my thinking. I was sick of revolving relationships. It was no good anymore. Enough already. No more. The cup was filled. Even if it meant never being in a relationship again, I wasn't going to have another bad one. That dream also helped me to see what I was doing wrong, how foolish I was being—especially in light of what I really wanted out of life. I was ready for change."

It wasn't long after this shift in thinking that Pamela met Oliver, the man who has been her permanent partner for over 20 years.

Michael: Michael had a similar experience. He is the steady, Rock-of-Gibralter type who runs a successful business as an electrician. Though he felt successful on the job, he described himself as "very unlucky at love." He had had a disastrous relationship with a live-in partner and then had fallen in love with Carol, dating her for over four years. During that time he saw her exclusively, but she continued a relationship with another man. Even though he knew this was going on, Michael never once talked to her about marriage or an exclusive relationship. Then things changed. He explains:

"The roommate I was living with was studying counseling. Every evening after he came home from school we would discuss his classes. I learned a lot from these discussions. After one of our talks, I made a big decision. I decided to stop accepting things just as they were if they didn't make me happy. I confronted my feelings for Carol and realized I was deeply committed to her. I had learned from my roommate's classes there should be a reciprocity of commitment for a relationship to be in balance. I decided to request this of Carol and, if she refused, to break off the relationship. I was not going to spin my wheels any longer. I also realized that I was tired of spending time at Carol's place and then going back to my place and not knowing if my things were there or here or in the car. The more I thought about both issues, the more I concluded I would be happier married. I finally said to her, 'I've had it. I don't like the situation we are in now. I'd be happier if we were married.' Carol said she didn't know if she was ready for a commitment; so I said, 'I'll give you 30 days to make up your mind. Don't call me unless you're interested.' On day 29, she called."

If your relationsickness is mild and you need only to recognize it to be on your way to putting it behind you, you are well on your way to completing Step One. Your journey to permanent partnership has only four more steps. You have known people who have had a shock that changed the way they valued life, who have read a book and felt, "Hey, there's a better way," remembered their dreams and reached for something better, listened to a lecture and took the inspiration to heart.[1] Such episodes expanded their world view and encouraged them to change the course of their lives. Pamela and Michael both experienced a profound gut-level shift in the way they saw themselves. They felt the energy and insight that enabled them to take immediate action. The realization and knowledge that something was deeply wrong spurred each of them to consider that they could make better choices and ready themselves for serious commitments. In a sense, insight and awareness were the cures for them. What about you? What are your dreams? Is recognition enough for you to make a profound change or do you need stronger medicine?

Regular-Dose Cure

For many people, the realization that there is a problem is not enough. In fact, it is just the beginning. It is the first piece of an ongoing strategy to overcome a negative view of their world, but they have personal resources and tools at their disposal that give them the capacity to self-cure. They have already solved a serious problem and can apply the same techniques and strategies to a new one. Their having lived through a successful experience gives them confidence that they can do it again. For example, after going through a 12-step program, someone who is a recovering alcoholic may use the same principles to combat other addictions—tobacco, sweets, feelings and even inappropriate people.

To outline and follow a recovery program without the aid of others is extremely difficult to do, yet several of the people we talked to had accomplished it. In fact, many found that four stages worked for them:

1. Observe what's going on and think things through.
2. Pay attention to thoughts remembering they control emotions.
3. Decide what actions need to be taken.
4. Put energy behind these decisions and follow through.

Stage Four is critical. Good intentions give us a jump start but that burst of energy only goes so far. As one person saw it, "I've made a big contribution to paving the road to hell." It's the continued energy put into action and follow through that makes the process a winner. Otherwise, intention is like a rocket that goes up but fails to burst. Grace was determined not to fizzle in her desire to buy a house.

Grace: Grace had been a compulsive eater most of her life. Although she sometimes was quite thin in appearance, food dominated her thoughts and she felt "fat" inside. After trying and failing with every new diet, spending all of her vacations at health spas and keeping a closet full of clothes ranging four sizes, Grace had almost given up on ever being what she considered normal. A turning point came when she decided to buy a house she loved. The catch was that she could only afford it with a roommate. She had avoided roommates in the past because she kept from being overweight by keeping very little food in her house. With a roommate, this was impossible. The house was beautiful and Grace wanted it so badly, she decided to get a roommate and self-cure from being a compulsive eater. She went out and bought every book she could find on the subject. She knew most of them were crash diets that would only lead to another vicious circle, but she found one that made sense to her. She followed its advice: recognize hunger; eat to satisfy it; stop when it's done. She also did the recommended exercises and had the self discipline to stick to the program. Within a year, food was no longer a major problem for Grace. She had her house, a figure she liked, and self-esteem from having solved a tough problem.

Grace was a skilled mathematics teacher who learned fast from her experiences. She explains how she tackled relationsickness:

"I didn't even realize that relationships were a problem for me until I found myself unable to break off with a man who regularly beat me up emotionally. My friends got sick of my complaining about him and then running back to him as soon as he would indicate the slightest interest. After several months of being miserable, the turning point came when he 'forgot' my birthday. I vowed another birthday would not go past with me being in such a one-sided relationship always ending up feeling hurt and disappointed. Fortunately, I had experienced overcoming addictions. I say 'fortunately' now, but at the time you're combating a compulsion, it's the worst feeling in the world. To say the least, it's not a lot of fun, but I knew from experience that I could do it and that I could do it alone, if you can call advice from books 'alone.' I read everything I could on the subject and followed the advice which struck a cord with me. Actually, it was easier than the first time I struggled with an addiction. This time I knew all that it took. I also knew I could do it. I made a well thought-out plan and, lucky for me, had the perseverance to follow it."

Grace was far more than lucky. Her previous success empowered her with greater confidence and self-esteem. She experienced overcoming a complex and painful problem and, therefore, had the skills to work on relationsickness on her own.

Do you have any such skills and personal resources that you can draw on when it's time for a change? Can you count on yourself to develop and rigorously follow a strategy to overcome relationship problems? Can you follow a plan that's mapped out in your own behalf? Do you keep your commitments to yourself? If so, all you need is the regular-strength dose and nothing stronger. If not, you probably would benefit from stronger medicine—the extra-strength dose. This dose involves the assistance of a qualified professional to guide you on the path of healing any wounds.

The Extra-Strength Dose Cure

For several of the people we interviewed, change would not come by first gaining insight and then developing a plan. That just wasn't enough. Many shared with us the belief that the reasons behind their relationsickness were so unconscious, so buried, that they simply felt compelled to retain old patterns even though they knew intellectually these patterns were self-defeating.

Tad: As Tad put it, "I knew the woman I was involved with was bad for me, but I knew just as clearly that anyone I would replace her with would be equally bad, no matter how hard I tried to remain conscious about my choice. I had always made decisions based on my instincts, which were usually pretty good. However, decisions involving women were a sorry exception. In the choice of lovers, they were terrible. The dilemma I faced, however, was that if I couldn't trust my instincts, what else could I rely on to guide me?"

Tad chose to go to a marriage and family therapist for help in decision-making about women. He vowed to stick with it until he could re-educate his instincts. Others choose to enlist the support of a psychiatrist, psychologist, social worker, teacher, support group, minister or rabbi. Helpers such as these assist a person in unraveling early life decisions which are no longer appropriate. Once these can be faced and released, the way is cleared for healthier, more realistic decisions to take their place.

Do not be frustrated if you discover that the best cure for you is to seek someone to help you make changes in your life. Not being able to understand by yourself what is going on that motivates you to self-deception and unhappiness is reason enough to look for guidance. If you have been abused or neglected in childhood, it is quite probable that you need outside help. Abuse can take many forms. The most obvious, of course, is physical, but for every child who has been physically abused, countless more have suffered emotional abuse. Emotional and physical abuse are often very hard for the victim to identify and re-experience alone. Ugly memories can be overwhelming.

Sarah: Sarah, a competent physical therapist in her early 30's, was distraught because she would allow no men in her life. In the middle of a conversation with her about abuse, her face clouded over, tears welled up, and her hands made a protective gesture over her chest as she pulled in her breath. The memories of a cruel stepfather flooded her entire body. "These memories are so painful I can only experience them a few minutes at a time." Sarah's stepfather had not only abused her and her mother by violently slapping them around while shouting epithets, but he also had run Sarah down with his car. It took her many visits with her therapist before she could even let herself remember these experiences. They were so filled with pain that she needed a trusted and competent ally to allow them to surface.

When you suspect you have a serious physical illness, you go to a doctor to have it checked out. Don't shortchange your psyche. If a commitment to permanent partnership is something you want in your future yet you find that, no matter how hard you try, it eludes you, why not seek the help of a qualified professional?

There are benefits that emerge from every problem. The ramifications of tackling one like relationsickness usually have unexpected, but wonderful, side effects. Michele had the need to take the Extra-Strength Dose in order to recover from her bout with relationsickness. For her, it all started with an undeniably bad relationship.

Michele: "I had had my share of bad relationships, sometimes one right after another, but it took my four-month marriage to Jim to make me realize things were not going to get better by trying to solve them on my own. I was angry and depressed. I had to change. But how? I had tried to improve my selection of men by being really careful before I would allow myself to get involved. But even though each time I thought in the beginning I had done better, there would come a point when I realized I had made another error. I'd gotten involved with someone who was incapable or unwilling to be a permanent partner. Of course, by then I was emotionally involved and to free myself was very painful.

"Finally, even though I'm a very self-disciplined person, I realized I couldn't do it alone. I was being driven by needs that were so unconscious they could only be identified with the objectivity of a trained professional. I needed the help of a teacher, a guide, someone to help me discover why I acted as I did, to hold my hand while I gave up old ways and to help me learn new ones. I was prepared to work hard with a therapist for the first time in my life.

"Giving up relationsickness and finding a permanent partner became the number one priority in my life. It became more important than my job, more important than my material possessions, more important than the comfort of retaining old habits. I committed to doing whatever it took to find love that was real and honest. For the first time in my life, I was emotionally and mentally determined to find a permanent partner. I found a great therapist who is trained in many disciplines, including transactional analysis, with whom I established a healthy, caring relationship. I committed to spending whatever resources—time, energy and money—the treatment would take.

"After spending a year and half in therapy, things began to click for me. I moved from hitting the rock bottom place of only being involved with men who weren't good for me to only being attracted to ones who were likely candidates for permanent partners. It wasn't long before I met and married my permanent partner. He is so much better than my wildest dreams! I'm glad I had to experience the pain which pushed me to get help and to get well. Plus, I found that as a side benefit to straightening up my relationships with men, I improved my relationships at work, with my family and with my friends. My life in general began to get clear and even beautiful for the first time."

Tad and Michele had success with the kind of therapy in which they straightened out their thoughts and feelings by talking things over with a qualified professional. Walter, an insurance company supervisor in his 40's, had a therapeutic experience that not only involved talking things through with a therapist but relied heavily on role-playing.

Walter: Walter described himself as "not able to love." He was overly critical of any woman friend, often had outbursts of anger, and had little capacity for warmth and affection. No matter how loyal his partner was, he would eventually drive her away. To conquer the root cause of his anger, Walter had to face the fact that his father, a respected scientist, had neglected him, over-criticized him, and demonstrated little caring or love. Admitting this, even though it was only to himself, was a hard thing for him to do. It conflicted with the previous story he had been telling himself and the world, that his father was a wonderful person. As he faced the truth—his truth—about his father, the hurt, anger and rage welled up inside him.

His therapist, trained in gestalt therapy methods, encouraged him to speak out to his father, who in Walter's imagination sat in an actual empty chair across from him. Several sessions culminated in his yelling all the hateful, hurtful things he felt inside. He also role-played his father and gained some insight into his point of view. Some insights brought Walter to bitter sobs, and his frozen feelings gradually began to thaw. None of this was done in the presence of his actual father. In addition, he learned from his therapist how to repeat this kind of release and integration any time he found himself getting unreasonably angry at someone's trivial misdeed. He would sequester himself in a private place and openly express his innermost feelings until the energy seemed to go out of the anger. All of this was done consciously and in a protected situation. Finally, after many sessions, he felt spent, as if the wind had gone out of his anger and he didn't have to struggle anymore. He reported, "I feel as if my soul has had a long, warm shower."

The end result of Walter's facing his anger and bitterness and working through it was that he was finally able to release his natural affection and become more open and accepting. He shifted from cold and aloof to warm and caring. This change made him much more attractive to emotionally healthy women. For Walter to get to this place took a large dose of the Extra Strength Cure.

Most of us who are relationsick would know whether we need a Small-Dose Cure, Regular-Strength Cure or an Extra-Strength Cure. How about you? Is insight enough? Can you go it alone and make the progress you need or do you need to seek competent professional help? If help is in order, see Appendix D for suggestions on how and what to look for to make your psychotherapy a success. There are helpful organizations in most communities such as Al-Anon.

Don't let strife and struggle discourage you. Very often the struggle with relationsickness forces people to put forth the energy, fortitude and dedication needed to get well. Simultaneously they learn many of the lessons they need in order to be successful permanent partners—a real serendipity! Change is rarely easy. You may think a Small-Dose cure is enough for you but find it doesn't work. If so, try the next level of cure. If you find you can't do it alone and need to take the strongest medicine outlined, don't be disappointed. Congratulate yourself on choosing the quickest, most reliable path for you. You will make it. One day you will be capable of finding and being a permanent partner. We feel sure of it.

The Power of Forgiveness

Whether a person needs a Small-Dose, Regular, or Extra-Strength Cure, old decisions, feelings and behaviors have to be laid aside. Many of the people whom we interviewed had had some kind of experience which had inhibited them from finding the love of their life and had generated such feelings as resentment, anger, hurt, inadequacy or sadness along with their poor choices. They had to acknowledge, understand and master these feelings in order to allow their more positive feelings of love and affection to radiate from them. Bottled up fear and resentment always blocks love and affection.

Almost all great religious traditions teach the importance of a forgiving nature. Indeed, forgiveness is an essential component of mental and physical health. In a sense, to be forgiving can be thought of as ultimately serving oneself. When we harbor grudges, resentments and deep hostilities, we also keep hurtful experiences alive and motivating us. Bitter thoughts, *no matter how justified*, do us far more harm than good. Our thoughts spark emotions which move us to action. Bitter thoughts can create a bitter life.

When we hold resentments from the past, again even though justified, the negative feelings do us damage. They stress us. They cause us to hold certain muscles tense and even to hold our breath. It's as if we store all of our negative experiences somewhere in our bodies, letting them keep a tight grip on us while destroying our sense of peace. All of this self-torture does little to remedy a bad situation or change the people involved. We need to let go of this stress and forgive the people who have wronged us, not necessarily for their sake, but for our own. To start doing this, we must face our negative behaviors and feelings and move beyond them. That's what transformation is about—shedding the old like a caterpillar emerging from its cocoon as a butterfly and becoming something new. Eventually, to find inner peace, we need to forgive those who have trod on our personhood, our dignity and our self-esteem. We must learn to see the past differently. We may need to get good and mad first and get help to harmlessly release the negative feelings, but why be stuck holding an ever-present bag of negative thoughts, emotions and mental pictures that only serve to torment us? *To change the outer world, the inner world must change first.*

For example, the real test for Walter's transformation came when he was able to go to his elderly and very ill father's bedside and comfort him by reading aloud from his father's favorite books. For the first time, he felt they were friends. And even if this were not the case, he felt he had created room in his life for warmth, affection and unconditional love. Forgiving his father's bad habits seemed a small price to pay for his own inner contentment.

The Use of Rituals for Healing

The practice of forgiveness and positive rituals often go hand-in-hand. Rituals hold symbolic meanings which speak to feelings and thoughts that can't be put into ordinary words. Our psyche deals with pictures and images which form complexities of meaning beyond language. We can design a ritual to symbolize a resolution of a past problem, a new beginning or a reinforcement of a newly formed belief or idea. Rituals speak to us far more deeply than words can reach.

Sarah: Sarah felt she needed to free herself from a resentment she had held for years against her mother. As part of her Regular-Dose Cure, she devised a ritual that she felt was appropriate for her purpose and situation. She went to a large neighborhood cathedral several times. Each time she lit a candle and sat quietly for half an hour repeating to herself forgiveness for what she felt was her mother's wrong-doing. She kept saying over and over to herself: "You did it out of ignorance and insensitivity, not malice. I release my resentment and forgive you." At first she didn't fully believe her words, but, eventually, she really heard and accepted them. When this happened, her hurt feelings dissipated and stopped interfering in her life. Later, Sarah described herself as feeling "lighter and brighter."

Diane: Diane finally accepted that she had an "imperfect" body which, along with her sexuality, she had been hiding most of her adult life. Though imperfect by Madison Avenue standards, her body was just fine. To act out her ritual, she ceremoniously burned all of her long, flannel nightgowns. "It was a strange and wonderful feeling watching all my hiding places go up in smoke."

Howard: Howard figured out that he had been programmed to be a workaholic. For his ritual, he invented a large basket that he placed near his office door—in his imagination, of course. Each day when he left his office, he also mentally left all his work, cares and unmade decisions in this basket ready to be picked up the next morning. For years before, he had taken all of his cares into his private life and never had "time" for love and family.

Mel: Mel recognized he had acted out his unfinished business with his mother on his wife. After having brought this all to light in therapy, he bought several helium balloons, wrote old behaviors on each, took them to the top of a nearby hill, and popped them one by one releasing the helium to the heavens. "With each balloon I felt like heavy weights flew off my shoulders!"

What Now?

The wounds that cause relationsickness can be healed. They are a curable disorder. Armed with insights as to how much outside help you need so that you can make your choice of an appropriate cure, you are on your way.

But be aware. Don't spin your wheels trying to change someone else. *Don't get caught in the trap of postponing your own happiness until someone else sees fit to change.* It's only a way to give up your own personal power. And, anyway, it's never likely to happen. Only you can take the first steps to heal any wounds that have caused you relationsickness. Only you can decide on the best cure. Remember that where you seem to be stumbling in life, you have the greatest potential for growth. When you release your pain and ready yourself for something much better to come your way, something much better will show up.

Questions and Exercises

Determining the Degree of Relationsickness: Think about each of the following questions carefully. Let them help you sort out how much you need to do or how much help you might require to recover from any degree of relationsickness that could be stopping you from a successful partnership. Feelings, behaviors and motivations that you don't understand often require some form of therapy.

1. Do I get very angry at another's transgressions and later realize they were fairly trivial (i.e., are my emotions out of sync with the reality/severity of the occasion?)

2. Are my feelings more easily hurt than others' seem to be?

3. Do I sometimes have a hard time knowing what I am feeling?

4. Do I sometimes have a hard time identifying why I feel the way I do?

5. Have I tried to *develop* a plan to change a habit and found I couldn't or wouldn't develop it?

6. Have I tried to *follow* a plan to change a habit and found I couldn't or wouldn't follow it?

7. Do I have the skills to self-cure?

8. Do I have the will-power to self-cure?

9. Do I have a support group of friends who will reinforce my efforts to heal?

10. Do the people I depend on for advice really help me improve my life?

11. Do my actions towards potential permanent partners surprise me (i.e., am I in touch with my motivators)?

12. Are there situations or memories which might influence my relationships that I don't fully understand?

13. Do I have uneasy feelings about my past experiences that make me suspect "something" I'm not in touch with might be influencing my present relationships?

14. Have former attempts at relationships resulted in several people saying the same things about my capacity for a relationship? What did they say? Do I believe it's true?

15. Am I ready to confront the truth about myself, my situation, and what I have to do in order to give up any relationsickness I think holds me back?

16. If so, here is my contract:

17. Here is the first action step I'll take:

Finding the right-dose cure for yourself could lead you to a whole new way of looking at life and your possibilities. Whether it's just awareness you need or a well thought-out plan or therapy, it's well worth your time and effort to heal any wounds that keep you from living life to its fullest.

ENDNOTE

1. For a list of helpful books, see Appendix C, "Helpful Books for Special Problems."

Chapter 4

Step 2:
Know What You Want

Luck is what happens when preparation meets opportunity.
Elmer Letterman

Remember what the introduction said? "Recognizing and feeling attracted to the right person is the trick"? How true it is. Buried deep inside each person are subconscious motives that may be misguiding. They shape our behavior until we send new, clear signals. We are indeed many selves who do not all agree with each other. Haven't you made a choice that a more enlightened part of you knew was not right? It's like sitting in front of something luscious but not good for you to eat, perhaps a piece of wonderful looking pie. Part of you says with relish, "Wow, I'm going to eat every crumb!" Another part says, "I've lost five pounds and I'm not going to stop my efforts now." Then a more crafty part enters the scene with, "Just take one bite. That won't hurt." Or, "Eat it, dear. It'll keep up your strength." Conflicts are often our inner selves having arguments. Unfortunately, the part that wins the battle often makes choices that are downright bad for us. Not *all* of our inner selves have our best interests at heart. They're just carrying out previous commands. Your task is to examine and change those commands.

As you progress with Step One and start healing any wounds, you'll find that many of the unhealthy motivations from your past will take their proper place in history and will no longer serve to push you in inappropriate directions. Remember that when we don't deal with past issues, they line up and knock at the door of our conscious minds saying, "I'm going to keep nagging you until you pay me some attention and put me to rest."

Getting Clear

You are responsible for developing an inner self that is on the side of what makes you the happiest—and, in the long run, the most fulfilled. You must empower this self and give it the authority it needs so it can deal properly with the other parts of your psyche. Large doses of self-esteem and self-confidence form a solid core of self-respect and competence and are the very best gifts to give yourself. Your spiritual core reflects what's good in you, what makes you shine. Sometimes the tarnish needs to be wiped away so that love and joy can sparkle through your eyes. Learn to want and do what feeds your soul.

"Be careful about what you want because you just might get it!" is an admonition which often rings true. It is amazing how many times we *do* get what we want. For that reason it behooves us all to learn to want what's best for us. It is in our own best interests to make an effort to get clear with ourselves by actually taking charge of our wants and desires in a conscious way. We're not talking about striving and straining but, instead, about being fully awake to our possibilities.

Since you are preparing yourself for permanent partnership, a critical step is for you to make fully conscious those qualities that earmark a good relationship—*not just any good qualities, but qualities good for you.* When you put on your thinking cap, quiet your mind and examine your experiences, you will begin to recognize what meets your needs, what you can respect and support in another person, what you can live with through thick and thin. On your life's journey, what kind of person do you really want to take along with you?

What We Don't Want

When a losing, inappropriate relationship has just ended and we are feeling the first pangs of "what happened?," it's natural to begin by being loud and clear about what we *don't* want. Unfortunately, this is the easiest part. The most difficult part for most of us is sorting out what we *do* want.

Rick: Rick was a genius at crunching numbers in a large insurance firm. He loudly expressed his resentment after a difficult, five-year marriage ended in a bitter divorce. He railed on and on about all the things wrong with his former wife. She was cold, dishonest, greedy, flirted with other men, etc. To the most minute detail, he knew exactly what he didn't like about her. He even woke up in the middle of the night wanting to vent his anger and frustrations. When asked what he *did* want in a life companion, he was stunned by the question. He'd never thought about it that way. He spent a couple of weeks mulling it over and finally wrote down some conclusions. He was asked to write down his full list and then reduce it to the three most important qualities. Then he was to reduce these qualities to three key words or phrases starting with the most important, then look at this list every night and morning. His list read: Loving, Honest, Intelligent. Many thoughts, ideas and mental pictures surrounded these simple words. This exercise had a profoundly positive effect on his next choice. Six months later, he had found a real permanent partner. He elaborated, "By really being clear with myself, I've gone from the very worst situation to one that couldn't be better; and I feel pretty lucky that I did it in just one leap. It's uncanny how Anna matches my list!" Within 18 months, Rick and Anna were married. A year later they joyously celebrated the birth of their baby daughter. Later, when Rick decided to look for a new job, he put the same method to work for him.

What We Do Want

The need to be clear and conscious about what you really want is true whether it's a job, education, vacation or permanent partner. As mentioned earlier, our unexamined, subconscious beliefs are often distortions or unrealistic fantasies—shadows gathered from the past. Then, without our conscious knowledge, these "shadows" compel us to behave irrationally and even destructively. On the surface we say we want a close relationship but subconsciously we still hold fears, resentments and beliefs. These fears, resentments and beliefs are stronger than our desires and serve to motivate our behavior. When this happens, the original program overrides the intellect. As a result, we may be blind to realistic standards and concrete, self-enhancing objectives. Most successful people have a clear picture about what they want out of life and love. This clarity gives the conscious and subconscious mind a chance to help with the search. In fact, our minds deal in pictures all the time. One reason it's important to focus on what we *do* want, is that it sends a clear signal to the mind. For example, if you say to yourself, "I don't want to think about horses," you won't be able to get horses out of your mind. If you want to think about elephants instead, tell your mind, "I want to think about elephants," and it will happen.

The people we listened to expressed universal qualities that they eventually were drawn to. Those looking for healthy, dynamic relationships looked for others who were nurturing, dependable, who respected them and who cared about their feelings. Marianne, whom we first met in Chapter 3, talks about what knowing what you want meant to her. We include a large portion of her interview [edited] here because she experienced so many beliefs, feelings, circumstances and attitudes common to others.

Marianne and Doug: "For me, knowing what I wanted started off with knowing where I wanted to live. I had to make a mistake first to help me get that very clear. When I left my first husband, I had no place to go. So I moved to a Southern state because my parents were there. But even though I loved having my parents close by, the place I moved to was wrong for me. Nobody knew me. Nobody cared. The things that I was interested in, nobody else was interested in. I would have to think through clearly where I would find a like-minded community. I needed *good*, free schools for my children. I needed an environment where the fact that I no longer had any money to speak of didn't matter so much. I could be recognized in terms of my education, my lifestyle.

"I decided a university town was the best place for me. University towns usually have good schools because people care. Also I wanted some place near a city, but some place with business opportunities diverse enough so that I could work but wouldn't have to commute and leave my children. Plus, I vowed no matter how much I had to spend, even if I had to work three jobs, I was going to have a house in a neighborhood. Once I was clear on what I needed, choosing a final destination wasn't that hard. It turned out to be on the West Coast. But once I got there I knew it was right.

"I moved in the car with the kids. I didn't have many possessions. No beds, no furniture, just a few things that meant a lot to me. It was scary.

"I met my second husband, Doug, five months after moving. I had gotten a part-time job from an ad in the paper and my boss invited me to a Christmas party at his home. I met a couple of single women who were fascinated that I had moved across the country with no job and no alimony. They couldn't imagine how anybody could take such risks. Two days later one of the women called me and asked if she could give my telephone number to 'a Jewish doctor.' My first husband had been a psychiatrist so my immediate response was, 'No thanks. I've already had one of those!' Then she explained it was her ex-husband. I couldn't believe what I was hearing. Her ex-husband! I was astounded but she assured me he was a very nice guy. She said she had never set him up before but she felt we would like each other. She was right. We were married 15 months later.

"The second time around, I could put into words—the way I could put into words where I wanted to live—*what I wanted in a man*. I wanted somebody as competent as I, somebody who was able to take care of his own life. I mean, the specter of the neediness of my first husband haunted me. But I wanted somebody who was as (it sounds so corny), but as fully a whole person as I. The marriage would be the whipped cream, the coming together.

"Doug is not only nice, he's kind and generous. He has a similar kind of outlook on life about what's important, what's not important. He has friends. I had overlooked that my first husband had no friends. He told me that was because he was so miserable about his first divorce. He told me it was because he wanted to be with me alone. Well, the second time around I would never accept that, whereas, at 21, I said, 'Oh, of course, poor baby.' The second time around it was very important for me to see what kind of a life this person made for himself. Did he live under a light bulb and wait for somebody to come and save him? Or was he a full person who had his own life, his own friends?

"Another thing very important was family. My first husband's family was as weird as he was and I did not recognize it. Of course, they weren't flaming crazies. They were a very nice, educated family so on the surface you wouldn't think that there was anything wrong. But, you know, his mother and father hadn't talked seriously for 25 years. The father always had a string of mistresses. He was very disapproving of his children, never supportive and warm. I didn't even know how to assess those things. The second time around, I wanted to meet my future husband's family. I was much more interested in seeing what kind of people he came from. And I didn't believe just words. I had to see it. I had to see it borne out.

"How else did I know he was *the* guy? Well, he would do certain things. For instance, I'd been teaching school but now a fifth year was required so I had to go back to college. He said to me the night before I started, 'By the way, why don't you call the kids' schools and put me on their emergency cards—just in case something happens to them and you're away.' It sounds like such a little thing. But I am the caretaker. I take care of people. I'd been taking care of myself since I can remember. I take care of everybody and it never occurs to me that I couldn't take care of myself. And he said, 'I'll take care of you.' I can't tell you what those words meant to me. And, after over 17 years, I still can't get used to the fact that somebody's taking care of me as much as I take care of him.

"I have learned much more appropriate boundaries of what is required of me. You can imagine somebody like me, given the proclivities I have, finding in my first husband the neediest person around. I mean, I could have put an ad in the paper and I don't think I could have done as well as my own radar. So, here's this person who . . . it was no trouble for him to take care of other people in this very normal way. Whereas my first husband may have wanted to be generous, but he didn't have enough left over to be generous. It took everything he had plus all of my efforts just to take care of himself, to get through a day. Here was somebody who was competent, who was sure of himself, who had energy, emotional energy, who was realistic about what I could do, what he could do, and whose idea of a relationship was that we both take care of each other.

"How would I advise people thinking about getting married again? I would advise them to get with a person that they trust and say, 'Look, I think I want to marry this person and I'd like to talk to you about it. Can we talk about what kind of a person I am and what my needs are?' I would advise them to have premarital counseling—like the Catholic Church has couples do. I'd try to find out things like whether this couple has ways of fighting, whether they know if they get into a fight there's a way of getting out of that fight. I'd find out what they believe in, if they both want to have children—big basic things. But what I'd really advise them to look at is how much they know about themselves and how much they think their needs are going to be met by the other person, and if they're seeing the other person clearly. Are they seeing the other as strong and dominating as I saw at 21 in that first marriage—which wasn't very realistic? I would tell them, 'Understand what you need and want and what you are getting in return for what you give.' Very importantly, I would want to see how much the other person liked them. Were they always trying to change them? Do they really just *like* that person? Do they get pleasure out of just the way they are rather than, 'If you would just dress differently,' or 'When we get married, I would love you to cut your hair.'

"Do they both have an idea, a myth so to speak, of what should happen to people when they're married and is this myth really in keeping with who this person is or not? Is it pure fantasy or is it realistic? What do they think is going to happen when they marry? What is this person going to do? There's one really great thing that I just never knew, I just never knew . . . but now my mother tells me it was always there in her marriage to my father. She points out to me how independent each of them is, how it never would occur to my mother to ask permission to go some place. She would say—out of courtesy and love—'Sweety, I'm going to have to be in a meeting all day.' But never, 'May I?' 'Can I?' *They should never let anybody undermine their authority or their autonomy or their personhood."*

Marianne's unhappy marriage certainly caused her to hit rock bottom (which many of us seem to need to do before we get the energy to make a significant turn around in our lives). However, eventually it pushed her to take risks and to make plans. She learned from her experiences and her mistakes. She knew what she wanted. She knew what she wanted for her children—the kind of school, the kind of neighborhood, the kind of home. She knew what kind of city she wanted to live in, work in and raise her family. She knew what she wanted in a partner—nurturing, caring, sensitivity, intelligence, respect, independence—and, to her great credit, she recognized these qualities and valued them when she saw them. It took courage and determination, but she empowered herself to be attracted to a man who was an appropriate permanent partner for her.

Major Components of Intimate Relationships

To begin to expand and clarify *your want list*, let's look at the characteristics of an intimate, quality partnership. One way to begin to sort it out is to examine the four basic components of any intimate relationship: appropriate nurturing and protection, problem solving, the ability to play together, and a mutually satisfying sexual exchange.

Appropriate Nurturing and Protection

The ability to be nurturing toward each other when the situation calls for it—to feel both supported and cared for.

We learn most of our nurturing patterns from our original family. As a consequence, you will likely nurture others in ways you were nurtured. You will also tend to attract the kind of nurturing you learned to receive. If your parents were warm and loving, you will probably find displays of affection easy. You will also expect it from others. Taking care of someone who hurts, cooking for someone, wiping a tear away, making sure the car is safe—empathizing, sympathizing, feeding, cleaning—are all part of nurturing and nourishing others.

Relationsick couples usually don't share the nurturing. Either there is little nurturing in the relationship, or one partner carries the load as was the case in Marianne's first marriage. When one partner carries the whole load, it leads to psychological game playing and one-up/one-down relationships. People who attain healthy partnerships share the nurturing. Remember that a clue to a healthy relationship is reciprocity. The caretaking is healthy (i.e., only when needed) and *mutual*.

Problem Solving

The ability to define and solve problems as they arise in everyday life.

We all know that life is just one problem after another. The seriousness of these problems ranges from, "What shall we have for dinner?" to "How shall we handle this devastating illness?" Couples who can't identify and solve problems together tend to avoid facing problems, to leave all the decision making up to one party, or to argue a lot without coming to any resolutions. (Note: Arguing in itself can be healthy if it leads to mutually satisfying resolutions.) As a result, problems go unsolved and resentments build. The most common arguments involve money, in-laws, children and sex, but any topic will do. In fact, the same topics often come up in arguments over and over again—like a CD on "repeat." It's not uncommon for relationsick couples to go into excessive debt, make poor decisions about schooling, housing, etc., and live with a host of unresolved issues—each of which weighs heavily on the relationship.

Whether or not you feel capable of defining and solving problems is related to your experience and education. Some of us are quite competent but have been taught not to trust our intellects. Somehow, our intelligence was put down and we don't trust it. For example, in earlier generations many young girls were discouraged from being smart for fear they wouldn't be attractive to men. Current research shows this tendency continues in subtle ways. For example, in school, the academic achievement of girls is given less attention and taken less seriously by teachers (who are likely to be unaware of their biases) than is the academic achievement of boys.[2]

Some of us simply haven't learned the skills of problem solving. In relationhealth, couples identify and solve problems together, bringing each partner's knowledge and expertise to each issue. They talk things over. They listen to each other. They gather facts and make choices. They attempt to achieve resolutions that benefit the most people in the family. When hard decisions are called for, they make them together. They refrain from making unrealistic assumptions about each other's mental abilities and capitalize on the fact that two heads are better than one. They benefit from the fact that synergy works.

The Ability to Play Together

The ability to have fun together—to laugh with each other and at common experiences, to be able to play together no matter how old we are.

A person's capacity to giggle, experience great pleasure and be joyous is linked to the person's capacity for fun as a child. You have seen the awe, openness, wonder, and sheer joy that a free-spirited child can express. To have fun, you need to be able to release these same abilities, be open to new horizons, new adventures, new curiosities, no matter what your chronological age. Relationsick couples may find themselves sad and unhappy a great deal of the time. They experience few belly laughs and often use facetiousness and sarcasm in the guise of humor. Such hurtful humor really smacks of contempt and is a sure inhibitor of lasting love.

Enjoying common activities and recreation, sharing laughter, and experiencing pleasure together are all parts of a vital partnership— of relationhealth. Permanent partners plan and savor their time to play together. If they don't have the time, they make it. They look forward to the healthy pleasures of life with zest.

Satisfactory Sex

The ability to relate sexually in mutually satisfying ways.

A good sexual relationship hinges on our attitudes and knowledge about our bodies, our beliefs about sex roles and stereotypes, our capacity for pleasure, our desire to give pleasure, our physical health, attentive listening, and some understanding of physiological and psychological male/female differences. Men and women *are* different. What would seem to come naturally is often a focus of discord and tension in a relationship. Sexual experience carries with it a load of responsibilities, some even health- or life-threatening. In addition, any early sexual trauma is like an ever-present scar forming a barrier that blocks the ability to experience true joy in sex.

More than likely, your sense of yourself as a sexual person developed early in your life. You may have heard messages about what it means to be a "little woman" or a "little man." Perhaps you heard messages about the beauty and wonder of bodies or what it means to be good or bad. Maybe you didn't hear much of anything about intercourse from your parents. Most people don't. But, if not, you probably gained attitudes and "knowledge" from TV, magazines, movies, peers and the locker room. Many young men report their first sexual experience was in conjunction with a "girlie magazine"—very different from having to deal with a live person with needs. No one goes without sex education, but it's the kind and quality that counts. Whatever your upbringing or penchant for following current sexual fads, partnerships are earmarked by mutual caring, respect and pleasuring. Permanent partners often plan for intimate times "just for the two of us."[1]

What role does chemistry play is all this? Of course, it's ideal for partners to feel excitement just to be near one another. However, chemistry has its down side. Any of us can have a strong feeling of sexual attraction to someone who is not good for us otherwise. When the other three components are not there, hot chemistry does not signal a lasting relationship. Again, with permanent partners, the feelings are best when they are mutual; when they can be talked about; when they are open; and, above all, when there is trust.

Here are some examples from clinical practice of how three different couples played out these four components:

Helen and Hal: Helen never had met anyone she had as much fun with as Hal. They loved playing together—hiking, boating, dancing—and had wonderful weekends. In addition, if she was ill or depressed, Hal always seemed to say and do the right thing. They enjoyed being physically intimate and felt satisfied most of the time. However, Hal overspent his income and had a sizable gambling debt. When Helen tried to talk to him about a budget or how to get out of debt, he turned her away with, "I don't want to talk about it now. We were having a good time and now you've spoiled it." In the components of nurturing, play, and sex, their relationship was fulfilling, but their inability to define and solve problems together eventually caused them to separate.

Tim and Shari: Tim and Shari had an almost opposite problem. Tim loved his job as an engineer. He was conscientious, hardworking, did the odd jobs around the house, took major responsibilities in their church and provided financial security. However, when Shari became seriously ill, he put a glass of water along with the doctor's phone number on the nightstand by her bed, then left to spend the day helping a relative repair a troublesome garage door. Shari described their sex life as "mechanical" and they had little in common when it came to playing together. She liked bicycling, music, plays, the beach. He liked an isolated mountain cabin where he could read. In fact, he claimed, "Reading my professional journals is one of my greatest pleasures. I thoroughly enjoy vacationing where it's quiet so I can read without interruptions." Tim and Shari had no problems meeting their mortgage payments, keeping their house in order and budgeting their resources. However, Shari felt that she did all the nurturing. Tim felt he rarely had a "real" holiday, and their sex life was dull and passionless.

Jay and Mary: In contrast, Jay and Mary enjoyed an exceptionally happy sex life. They listened carefully to each other, shared what they liked most, and took a certain pride in making each other happy. If either of them needed nurturing, the other one was right there. Here again, they listened to each other and respected each other's nurturing style. Mary liked tender, loving care and knowing someone was there if she had needs. Jay mainly felt nurtured if Mary was on his "team." When he had a bad day, an illness, or just needed support, he wanted to know she was on his side and she usually was. Mary, however, would not help to solve problems. She acted childlike, as if she just didn't know anything and always put the burden on Jay. He had to make all the decisions (and take the blame) about money, mortgages, cars, furniture, school, etc. He also had to plan their playtime and vacations. Because she gave little input, she often complained that they never did anything or went any place where she really wanted to go. Jay and Mary functioned together very well when nurturing or sex were appropriate but had many unresolved issues around play and identifying and solving their problems.

Looking at their relationships from the point of view of the four major components of intimacy helped the above couples pinpoint where they needed to focus the healing necessary to make their relationships whole and healthy. If you seek a permanent partner who is more of a positive match in all four of these areas to begin with, you certainly have a head start on permanent partnership.

Personal Needs

Now begin to take an even deeper look inside yourself. As human beings, each of us has many needs to fulfill. We have emotional needs, physical needs, spiritual needs, mental needs, economic needs, aesthetic needs, etc. These needs can be normal, genuine, reasonable and call for legitimate fulfillment. However, some of us learn to be excessively "needy" people. This is true when one partner needs constant emotional support but is unable to give any in return. Usually when this occurs, one person drains the other. Here again, as in all aspects of appropriate permanent partners, *mutuality* is the key. Both parties need to be able to give and receive fulfillment. How are you at giving and receiving? What are the needs you want most to be met in a relationship? Every single need certainly doesn't have to be fulfilled by your partner—that would be a very shallow, friendless existence—however, for a close, continuing relationship to work, certain basic needs should be primarily met within that relationship. And it behooves you to know what those needs are for you.

Values

Whether or not you've thought about it consciously, you have your own values. Values center around what we believe in—our religious and spiritual beliefs, our feelings about the Earth and the environment, our need to do good for other people, our precious possessions, our sense of ethics and integrity. For example, a religious background may be part of your roots, your heritage. What compromises and changes are you willing to make?

Mickey: Mickey had related to many men who did not share her Jewish background. She did not consider religious affiliation important. However, when she hit rock bottom and then became ready for permanent partnership, it became clear to her that she deeply valued her religious heritage and wanted to be able to share its traditions. "I think, too, it's more a way of communicating. Traditions and customs don't have to be explained. They're just part of our common experience."

Dora: Dora was also crystal clear about her values and priorities. Without hesitation, she wrote:

1. God
2. Family
3. Having creative work
4. A healthy planet
5. Ballet dancing

When she evaluated whether or not someone was an appropriate permanent partner for her, she carefully noted that person's values in these areas.

Our values become the driving force for how we set our priorities in life. They determine how we use our life's time, a precious commodity. What do you believe in strongly enough that compels you to want to live with someone who shares, or at least understands and respects, your values?

Wanting What's Best

To set out firmly on the road to relationhealth, learn to want what is best for you. Then, when you have met your quality partner, you will experience a continuation of the healing process. A relationship with a person appropriate for you is healing in itself. For example, you will learn how to be more intimate and more committed when you are partners with a person who is at ease with these attributes. Veronica, a reserved woman who worked hard to become a registered nurse, experienced this phenomenon full force:

Veronica: "Mark is very committed to our relationship. He was from the beginning. It was like he *also* was tired of looking and being on his own and struggling with relationships. Also, he comes from a family who keeps commitments in relationships. This is the kind of background that I come from, too. Even though ethnically our backgrounds are different ends of the world from each other in many ways, we are very much alike in terms of family structure, in terms of belief about commitment to making things work, about helping each other achieve individual goals as well as collective goals. This was comfortable for me. It was reassuring that I knew I was important in our relationship. From the outset, I did not have to worry or to even think about whether or not there were other people he was involved with. That was nice.

"Our relationship nurtures me a lot. It's a very solid framework that keeps me grounded. Not restricted, but grounded. I know what he expects of me and he knows what I need. I can predict how he is going to respond to things because he is fairly consistent. I don't have to worry about him coming from left field. Or if he does, it's in response to something that's a trigger point and is predictable."

You can see from Veronica's experience that what is right for one person may not be what is right for another. There are many different ways to achieve relationhealth. We all have different "lessons" to learn and issues to resolve. You need to get very clear about what *you* want. To be clear, you must understand what makes up an intimate relationship. You must know what needs of yours have to be met. You must understand what you value above all else and not compromise your standards. But you also need to identify and distinguish "negotiable" from "non-negotiable" items.

Danell: Danell's needs were different from Veronica's, but she was very clear about what she wanted in a life partner. "Above all else he must be someone I can respect from the beginning. I learned the hard way that I can't turn someone else into a 'Good Guy.' Maybe Good Guys are born. But I know now that being respectable, trustworthy, having personal warmth and integrity, liking and respecting women, and being physically clean are very high items on my list."

You are responsible for becoming clear about what you want. Only *you* can take the steps necessary to change how you see the world and thus change how the world sees you. This is just a beginning. You are shifting your thinking from what subconsciously you've learned to believe you want, to an intelligent assessment of the kind of person you could love and respect, who would meet your needs, who shares your values, and with whom you could build a rewarding, long-lasting partnership. We tend to get what we believe we deserve. That's been the story of too many couples not to be taken seriously. When you are clear about what you want, you have a much better chance of recognizing it when it walks into your life.

Questions and Exercises

My Partner Profile: Begin to construct a picture of your perfect partner.

First, be very clear about any tendencies you have to be attracted to a clone (or the opposite) of your father or mother—especially if they were unsatisfactory partners themselves or lowered your self-esteem in any way. You started this process in the previous chapter. Add here any additional insights you have gained. Be clear on what you "wanted" in the past if you know it is not good for you now.

Now commit to cultivating the ability to make better judgments about the *suitability* of a partner—one that is more substantive, more enduring. Just what kind of a person is really appropriate for you? Write down what you really *want* in a permanent partner.

In the group we studied, there were qualities that seemed universal. People looking for healthy, dynamic relationships looked for others who were nurturing, dependable, who respected them, and who cared about their feelings. Did your description of what you want now have any of these qualities? If so, you are probably on the right track.

The Appropriate Person for You: To continue to develop your picture of the appropriate person for you, think about each of the areas listed below that are the four major components of any intimate relationship. Write down what you want from your lifelong mate. Just thinking about it isn't enough. Write it down. You can always come back and add to your list later as you gain new insights and understandings.

Appropriate Nurturing and Protection:

Problem Solving:

Ability to Play Together:

Ability for Mutually Satisfying Sex:

Know Your Needs: Now look back at what you wrote in the four major components of a partnership. What are your needs in each of these areas? Add what needs must be met in each of the four components. For example, do you want emotional support? Do you want your intellect respected or challenged? Do you want to be recognized as a sexual person—as a man or woman of integrity? Be specific.

As you think about yourself and your needs, ask yourself:

Am I an excessively "needy" person?

How must I adapt my needs to distinguish what of my expectations are realistic given:

a) who I am; and

b) what is available in the outside world?

Think about:

What emotional needs do I want met?

What physical needs?

What spiritual needs?

What mental needs?

What economic needs?

What aesthetic needs?

Any others?

Know What You Value: Consider what your five most important values are—the qualities and issues that you hold dear above all others, the values you do not want to live life without.

What are yours? Rank them in order of importance.

1.

2.

3.

4.

5.

Do you look for partners who hold the same values?

Now make any additions to what you are looking for in a permanent partner. Make the changes—additions and deletions—that have crossed your mind since your first description. Don't shirk this job. It may seem like hard work or too much bother but it could be one of the most important pieces of writing you have ever done.

Keep looking at your final description as you progress through the Matching Process. Change it to suit any new insights you might gain. Once you have it in a near final form, boil it down to three or four qualities. Look at it every day. Occasionally think about the kind of people you've let yourself be attracted to that weren't good for you. Use language that clearly places them in your past. "I used to really like_____ ." "I remember when I was attracted to _____ ."Then focus on your new images. Notice the differences. Feel good about the clarifications you've made for yourself. You now know what you are looking for and are beginning to send the correct instructions to your brain to help with the search.

ENDNOTES

1. cf. Eric Berne M.D., *Transactional Analysis in Psychotherapy*, Grove Press Inc., NY, 1961, pp. 128-130 and *Sex in Human Loving*, Simon and Schuster, NY, 1970, p. 167. Also see, Dorothy Jongeward, Ph.D., "A Compatibility Profile," *The Marriage and Family Counselors Quarterly*, Volume X, No. 1, Fall, 1975, California Association of Marriage and Family Counselors, Los Angeles, CA.

2. The AAUW report "How Schools Shortchange Girls: A Study of Major Findings on Girls and Education," commissioned by American Association of University Women's Educational Foundation and researched by the Wellesley College Center for research on women. A joint publication of the AAUW Educational Foundation and National Education Association, 1992.

Chapter 5

Step 3:
Be What You Seek

❤ ───────────────────────────────────── ❤

The highest reward for a person's toil is not what they get for it, but what they become by it.

John Ruskin

If you've ever experienced a hurtful relationship, you may have thought long and hard about what attracted you to it in the first place. Many things attract us to other people: looks, voice, mannerisms, the way they move their bodies, and even the way they smell. In fact, on the basis of recent studies showing the attraction of hormones called pheromones, perfume companies can exploit this notion commercially. But, even deeper than the way we smell, more profound motivations pull us toward others like magnets. These kinds of attractions occur at a whole different level and the remedies are not that easy to "sell."

The people we attract into our lives often have something to teach us. Whether these "lessons" seem to be for better or for worse, it is possible to learn a great deal about ourselves from others. Both negative and positive experiences hold nuggets of wisdom, if we'd only pay more attention to the messages. Rather than allowing things to happen randomly, we suggest that you examine what you project (seeing yourself in others) and what you admire (qualities in others that you respect) to accelerate your growth. Eventually, you can call those qualities that seem so special in others your own. You can "Be What You Seek." Clearing away as many negative projections as you can helps you achieve a higher consciousness about who you are.

Learning Through Projections

We can be drawn to people who compel us to examine who we are, who, through the phenomenon of projection, give us many opportunities to discover our innermost secrets—our subconscious selves. When we are projecting, we are seeing ourselves in others. We attribute the thoughts, feelings and beliefs that originate in our own minds to them. We see others as having those thoughts, feelings and behaviors. What disturbs us about another person often allows us to discover a disturbance deep inside ourselves. Our projections come from thoughts, feelings and beliefs that, for whatever reasons, we deny. Rather than confront these inner "gremlins," it seems easier to keep them buried and only recognize them in others. The gremlins may eat away at our guts, orchestrate our feelings, fuzz our thinking and blur our vision, but how many of us are willing to confront them for what they are?

When you are serious about personal growth, projection is a great tool for self-knowledge—for facing our gremlins. Once you muster up the courage, the people in your life, especially family, can help you face these inner issues. They don't have to do anything but be there. Yes, relationships offer one of the greatest potentials for growth, but fear and ignorance can keep us from going through the growing pains.

Seeing Ourselves in Others

At times we dislike, are mad at, or fear in others exactly what we are capable of ourselves. Qualities such as lying, cheating, anger, lust, meanness, greed and even cruelty are distasteful to admit. In fact, it's hard to see a fault in someone else that we don't possess to some degree ourselves. You have heard that "it takes one to know one." How true! Similarly, if we do not have the fault, we tend not to see it in others. There is no "charge" on it, by which we mean that the behavior doesn't upset us. We may look at someone and think they have a quirk, but it doesn't really bother us; we don't get distraught.

People with whom we have close contact, like our families, often serve as wonderful and sometimes astonishing "growth helpers" by being our mirrors and reflecting us back to ourselves. The projection of our negative traits onto others makes it possible to "see" our own behaviors—to see what's inside us, what we're capable of—like a movie on a screen. We can see clearly those behaviors we've carefully hidden from our own view. They are not hidden from others, mind you (they know!), but from us.

This phenomenon is happening to us all the time, saying "use me, use me," but it's all too easy to get mad at the people "out there" and not recognize that it's our own personal movie that is going on and *we're* the ones who are mad. When we say of someone, "He's always angry," we can very well be disowning our own anger and seeing it in someone else. Jealousy is often a projection. A sense of "I'm afraid my spouse will cheat on me" may belie our own "unbelievable" urges. We even project ourselves on inanimate objects. Have you ever hollered at your stupid car for running out of gas?

Those parts of us that we tuck away in our blind spot have great stories to tell us about ourselves. If we can learn to "see" these behaviors, embrace them as our own and then release them to the universe, it lightens our load considerably.

Murphy spent a lot of time complaining about his boss. His boss was a controlling so-and-so and he was sick and tired of it. When he turned this thought inward and asked himself, "Could I possibly have high needs for control?," he burst into a broad grin. Of course, he did! At a dinner gathering, Tess felt anger and disgust toward a man whom she "saw" as trying to be the life of the party. When she turned this question inward, it was pretty clear to her that she was the one who wanted to be the life of the party. With this realization, she laughed and, shaking her head with a smile, enjoyed the feelings of her frustration lifting from her.

Bringing what's subconscious—what we've hidden from ourselves—to our conscious minds can further our healing. While it might be shocking and even sad, it is most often amusing. It's amazing what a little awareness and a sense of humor can accomplish.

How do you go about doing this? The answer is simple but, again, not always easy. It needs to become a conscious practice. Every time you see something "wrong" in another person, something that disturbs you, go inside like Murphy and Tess did and look for that same trait or behavior in yourself. Ask, "Could I possibly be the one who is angry (depressed, controlling, mean, guilty, confused, dishonest, arrogant, acting stupid)?" Do your best to be honest. Usually you'll know if you have hit upon the truth. If you think maybe your imaginings have gotten out of control, talk them over with a trusted friend—someone who knows you well, sees you for who and what you are, and accepts you. In some instances, this may need to be a trained therapist. For example, if fear persists, you may need a qualified professional to assist you.

Once we own up to the rejected parts of ourselves that seem too negative to admit to, the tendency lessens to see others falsely. Our vision clears. We shift our perception of others and see them more clearly for who they actually are. The practice of looking in our "mirrors" and searching for the truth about ourselves is a fertile field for growth. This practice takes some determination but has great rewards.

Lee: Lee had been working at using the concept of possible projections to shed more light on what she called the shady side of her own behaviors. She had married and divorced the same person twice.

One evening she attended her regular study group where she and three other people had been meeting weekly for several months. When she entered the room and sat down, she noted that she had a strong negative feeling about one of the women who was chatting with the man across from her. She thought to herself, "She's always acting like a know-it-all." As was becoming her habit, when she felt annoyed by someone else's behavior, she went inside herself and asked, "Do I act like a know-it-all?" It occurred to her right away that she usually dominated these meetings. When she wasn't, she wanted to. Just this realization amused and amazed her. But, in addition, it gave her a great sense of relief and allowed her to monitor her behavior.

When we talk about learning from projections in order to gain more insight, we are encouraging you to become more aware of your own reality, to *pay attention to your own tendencies*. It is very often a relief to recognize and acknowledge—to bring to your consciousness— something negative inside yourself that you had not acknowledged before. And, believe it or not, it's sometimes even funny.

But there is another side to this same coin. We really are each other's teachers! In addition to learning about our negatives by looking for ourselves in others, we can also make personal gains by looking for positive traits. Clearing away projections can help us get to what we admire. We can observe those traits we admire in others, but believe we don't possess, and then bring them to maturity in ourselves. When we face our darker side and consciously develop admirable qualities, we open ourselves to new possibilities for being high-quality permanent partners. We take an active part in the process of becoming whole.

Learning from Admirations

There are many ways we can bring our fragmented selves together and become more whole. "Be What You Seek" is about just that— becoming whole. It's about putting our pieces back together again. It's about developing pieces we weren't aware we had. If we are incomplete ourselves, we are likely to attract others who are incomplete. Men and women who seek partners to "fill up their own emptiness" or "get someone to help them out" or "make their own life bearable" or who play the Dominant-Submissive Game have not yet learned how to be true partners. Rather than seeking a "better half" which can only lead to disappointment, focus on developing a "better-half" within. Real partnership implies give and take. You can't give if you are excessively needy. You can't take if you've learned to reject what others try to give you.

It takes a whole egg and a whole sperm to create a new life. If either the sperm or egg is incomplete, the process fails. The same idea holds true of human partnerships. Two whole people are needed to make one healthy permanent partnership. Susan's story illustrates how the principle of "Be What You Seek" and the quest for wholeness operated for her. Even though it took place over 18 years ago, it has as much relevance today as it did then.

Susan: Susan is a clear thinking, ambitious woman, who practices setting goals. She had two major goals. The first was to be financially secure. The second was to meet and marry a wonderful man who would be her life partner. She had grown up in a poor family, did not have any specialized schooling, and, for a long time, felt that the way to achieve financial security was to marry into it. It's not that she intended to compromise on the other qualities she sought in a mate: honesty, nurturance and commitment. But she did think it might be just as easy to find a well-established man who was wonderful as one who was poor and wonderful. The problem was that Susan was not meeting men from backgrounds much different from her own. She worked as a clerk in a back office and rarely met men on the job. So she asked herself, "How can I tap into the caliber of people who make good livings and who are lovable and respectable. What qualities do successful people possess that I don't? How can I set about being these things myself?"

Susan went to work on being what she sought. For her, this meant first joining a church group. The social aspect of religion had been an important part of her childhood, but one that she had left behind when she left home. She decided to rediscover this part of herself and took the step. She enjoyed her group immensely, feeling as if a part of her had "come home." This gave her the confidence to make another change: Susan changed professions. She felt that her job did not bring her into contact with enough people who fit the ideal qualities she was seeking. So, Susan went into real estate sales with the intention of focusing on larger, better homes. She reasoned that she would be making contact with wealthy clients who just might introduce her to a wealthy man. She took the training she needed and further developed her abilities and style. She became more open and honest, dependable, considerate, assertive and smart. These were qualities she'd admired in others. She loved her work.

To her own astonishment, Susan became a millionaire in her own right. She not only had financial security—her first goal—but she also met and married a wonderful man—her second goal. However, her plans had taken a surprising twist. The man with whom she fell in love and married had not been introduced to her by her clients and was not exactly wealthy. But even so, he played a big part in her achieving her need for security. He became her biggest cheerleader. He was her major supporter and comfort during the tough years of building her career. It paid off. She opened her own real estate office, now has a large number of people working for her, and is known as one of the most successful businesswomen in her state. A wonderful partner with whom she could share her journey facilitated her personal success. Susan became what she sought in a most profound way.

Veronica and Mark: Veronica, whom you met in Chapter 4, learned to be more of what she admired in others through her relationship with Mark. In her words: "Mark is painfully honest. He's not going to tell me something that's not the way he sees it. I find that hard to live up to, but I'm learning how to from Mark's example. Even though I can't do it myself all the time, I'm doing it more and more. I stop myself now when I start to gloss over things. I've had a tendency to make things look nicer than they are—easier to swallow. Mark is very straightforward and never slants the truth, so I always know where I stand. For better or worse, I always know where my feet are. That's wonderful for me because I had had awful relationships and had a hard time trusting anyone—especially men. Mark's being consistently honest is a pillar that anchors my ability to trust him. I know that there is nothing hidden because he consistently pushed even very uncomfortable issues to the surface quickly."

Veronica, a nurse by profession, also rediscovered her ability to be warm and affectionate while nursing her new friend, Mark, through the ordeal of a broken leg. "The three months that we lived together while Mark was mending his broken leg were wonderful. I would go to work and he stayed home hobbling on his leg and doing the home projects he had put off for years. The best part was that we nourished each other emotionally on a continual basis. My letting my warmth come through was reciprocated by his showing caring for me. This in turn activated my ability to be caring toward him and it kept escalating until we both were enveloped in the wonderful sensation of being loved on a deeper plane than either of us had experienced before. Just the affection we showed each other made this unpressured time together absolutely wonderful. We had both grown up in close, affectionate families and had missed the experience of just knowing daily that things were okay. There was, in addition, much, much more than affection that we shared during this time. It was a terrific beginning, one that I never in my wildest dreams would have predicted."

By interacting with and learning from Mark, Veronica continued developing her own high-quality traits as she moved toward greater wholeness and more love in her life.

Matt: Matt is an out-going, pleasant-spoken man who gives the impression of being sincere and continues to study toward his degree in chemistry, knowing that it would enhance his career opportunities. Matt sums up his experience with relationships like this: "I'm glad now that I had to face negative relationships, although at the time I would have said that it was a miserable state to be in. However, I can look back now and be grateful that I was forced to confront the deficiencies in who I was and how I was behaving. I like myself so much better now that I am living the way my soul wanted me to live. I can barely recognize the person I was in those days. Being in a very disturbed relationship, wanting to recover from it and be able to find a mate and have a family forced me to change the priorities in my life.

"I used to spend my summer weekends partying in the Hamptons [a resort area on Long Island]—just living it up. For me, when I made my decision to change, living my values meant joining a Bible study group and giving up my weekend excursions. The group met on Saturdays. I'm now back at the Hamptons on the weekends, but I'm having a good time with my wife and two sons. My wife is the sister of one of the members of the study group. We met six weeks after I joined and were married eight months later. Doing my best to live out those values that are important not only led me indirectly to her, it has helped me be a better father to my sons. I feel that I teach them how to be a person with high self-esteem by example and not just words."

In rare instances, incomplete people may force each other to grow in positive ways. But, far more often, such relationships drain our energy and eventually sour our spirits. Instead, cultivate in yourself the values that you seek in others. You will not only find your spirit soaring but also increase your personal appeal.

On your own personal journey, if you desire positive qualities in another person such as honesty, dependability, trustworthiness, integrity, tenderness, warmth, humor, joy, look to see if you manifest these qualities yourself. If not, it is likely that they lie dormant in you. We often admire in others exactly what we are capable of ourselves. When we say, "I wish I could be more like him. He is so warm and affectionate," we may be seeing potential qualities with which we've lost touch—qualities which don't seem to be part of our current repertoire of behaviors. If you want affection from a mate, you have to be able to give affection. If you want nurturing, you have to be nurturing. If you want fidelity, you have to give fidelity. If you want intelligent decision making, you have to be able to give intelligent input into decisions. If you want emotional intimacy, you have to be capable of emotional intimacy. If you want respect, you have to be respectful. If you want honesty, you have to be honest. This is an essential step for growth. As you keep working on it, your possibilities will continue to unfold. Other people who have these qualities are around you all the time. Learn from them. Read books. Take seminars. See a counselor. Your personal power, self-confidence and esteem will mushroom and multiply.

It's amazing. If you are like the partners interviewed, your self-esteem is a critical component of your success or failure in relationships. When you feel good about yourself, the world is likely to find you much more attractive—attractive to the right kind of people. When you don't, it's another story. You may still be attractive but attractive to someone who needs to make you better or keep you down, embarrass you or punish you. Without exception, the route that permanent partners take from unhappy to happy relationships involved focusing on the behaviors they valued. Right now, write down the top five qualities that you value most in a potential mate.

1.
2.
3.
4.
5.

Now think about how these qualities describe—or don't describe—you.

Honesty and Commitment

All the permanent partners interviewed listed honesty—a basic requirement for intimacy—and the ability to commit as two of the top five qualities most important for lasting relationships. Considering the importance of these two qualities to any successful partnership, it's not surprising that they were included. If you did not include them on your list of what you value most, you may want to re-consider. Naturally, you have the best viewpoint of your own "wants" but you will find that honesty and commitment are a must for those aspiring to lasting, growing love.

If these values are important for you to develop, start practicing the values you seek in daily situations with friends, neighbors, co-workers. Mollie told us about practicing honesty and commitment by keeping a promise to a friend. This may seem like a tiny step, but, for Mollie, even a simple commitment took great effort.

Mollie: Mollie is a puzzlement. She is cover-girl pretty with dark red, straight hair and deep blue eyes. She's smart and talented. In addition to being a successful financial planner, Mollie plays the piano and sings well. With all this, she lacks self-esteem and confidence. She seems absolutely oblivious to the pleasing image she presents to the world, often acting as though she were unworthy of love. Before she met and married Jake, she rarely dated. She was too shy to appear available. Instead, she projected an image of aloof coolness. Her few relationships were with men who were overly aggressive and seldom trustworthy.

Mollie was fed up with the kinds of relationships she was drawn to. The beginning of change for her started when she decided to break up with Don, a domineering man she been with for almost two years. Three weeks after she told him it was over, she took another courageous step. She agreed to meet a woman friend at a singles' dance. As she tells the story, she would never have been able to carry through her decision had she not made a promise to join her friend. Keeping this commitment opened the door to meeting a trustworthy man.

"I drove around the parking lot nine times trying to get the courage to go inside. My friend had told me that great guys went to these parties, but I was so scared, all I wanted to do was go home. I said to myself, 'I said I would attend. She trusts me to keep my word, so I will.' I finally got the courage to go in. I parked the car and started toward the door. A man was on his way out. I asked him if this was the singles' party. He said 'yes, but it's a terrible party.' Why didn't I go with him for a drink instead of going in? This really scared me. Again, if I hadn't promised my friend to meet her there I would have definitely turned around and gone home. I had reneged on promises to her and others before, but this time a little voice in my head kept saying, 'Keep your promise.' So I climbed the stairs, took a deep breath, and walked in.

"There were two tables to sign in. One for women. One for men. I walked to the one for women and filled out a card that the man behind the table handed me. I was so nervous that I got giddy and filled in the requested personal information with nonsense. For example, I filled in the schools attended with 'U. of Timbuktu.' Then I went in search of my friend. I couldn't see her in the crowd. I later found out that she had spotted me and went off to find a male friend that she wanted me to meet. By the time she had found him and brought him back to where I was standing, I was talking to Jake. He had crossed my path almost immediately as I had started to enter the crowded room. My first thought when I saw him was, 'He must be a jerk; he's too good looking to be nice.' But to my surprise, he *was* nice. He carried the conversation at first because I was too nervous to talk. Later it became easier to talk because he was so comfortable to talk to.

"I felt uneasy about having filled in the card at the door with misinformation, so I paid special attention to being honest with Jake. In fact, I even admitted to him how hard it had been to come to the party. He seemed surprised and then told me about his own insecurities, which, in turn, surprised me. Talking about feelings right from the start helped me relax and realize that underneath his good looks, Jake was a shy person who had self doubts, too. This made me feel less awkward.

"He invited me for coffee after the dance, but I felt I had to turn his offer down because I had promised to go out with my friend. I explained the situation and how commitments should be kept. He seemed to understand and respect that. We agreed to see each other the following Sunday.

"I thought Jake was good-looking the first moment I saw him, but no bells went off. It took me almost a year to realize how much I loved him. We were married 10 months after that. I think that the most important part of our relationship was that I discovered that I could really trust Jake. But I had to know inside first that he could really trust me. He'd go off alone on vacation and I knew that not only could I trust him while he was away, but that I could trust him to come back. He gave me lots of space, but I kept gravitating closer and closer to him because I could sense he was different. In fact, this whole relationship was so different from the traumatic, high-intensity, hurtful ones I'd had before.

"I'm glad I went to that party. I'm glad I had the courage to keep my promise to attend in the face of how scared I was. As I think about the changes I made between being with Don and meeting Jake, I realize that my relationship with Don was so awful, it made me determined not to make the same mistakes again. I wanted somebody different and I wanted to be different.

"Being the kind of person who I wanted in someone else took effort on my part. I had to practice being honest and keeping my commitments in order to find a committed guy. I also needed to practice risk-taking. The risk I took seems to be a small one, but it turned out to be significant. I never would have met Jake otherwise. I never would have had this wonderful marriage."

Mollie demonstrates how "Be What You Seek" works. She became a person of her word in order to find a person who kept his word. Mollie's story is just one example of the many permanent partners who practiced being the kind of person they sought. Many of the people interviewed felt that taking the step of being in touch with the values that were at their innermost core and monitoring their behavior on a daily basis to make sure it was in harmony with these values, made their lives work better in many ways. Not only did they find the "right" people gravitating toward them in their social arenas, they found business and family relationships shaping up as well.

Louise and Nick's story illustrates the fundamental importance of these same values of honesty and commitment. Including their story poses a dilemma. The reason is simple. When Louise met Nick, he was married. If there is one single source of pain reported by relationsick people who achieved relationhealth, it is involvement with a married person. Many, many of them, in discussing the role that rules played in guiding their behavior, expressed the wish that they had followed a rule saying "never have an affair with someone who is married." A prime symptom of lacking the values of honesty and commitment is to become involved with a person who is emotionally unavailable. Doesn't a married person courting a single person demonstrate a lack of honesty and commitment? But Louise and Nick's story has a different twist that not only attests to human frailties but also to their abilities to learn, grow and change.

Nick and Louise: Louise is not beautiful. However, she is extremely attractive. When she walks into a room, the way she carries herself, wears her clothes and speaks radiates self-confidence.

Nick expresses his sense of being drawn to her, "I picked Louise out of a room of 40 people because the image she projected was so attractive. I even noticed how she used her hands—something I had never done before."

"I like good-looking women," Nick admitted, "and there was no shortage of them around when I met Louise. But she stood out in a crowd. There was something about her that was very special and very appealing."

Louise had experienced her share of relationsickness. "Before I met Nick I had terrible relationships with men—not that I didn't have lots of men in my life, because I did. I would sometimes have three or four or five serious relationships going simultaneously. But I wasn't honest with any of them. I would play the old game of telling Peter, 'I'm going to see my mother for the weekend,' and go off with

Paul. I told myself that I did this because I didn't want to hurt anyone. But, in fact, the truth was that I needed the security of having lots of men in my life. It meant I didn't have to get really close to any one of them but could always have someone around when I wanted.

"That was fine until I got pregnant and wasn't sure who the father was. An unwanted, irresponsible pregnancy was a real shaking-up point for me. It hit me like a bombshell. I had to face the fact that I was no longer just screwing up my life, I was also screwing up another human life. I lost the baby but the feelings about the irresponsible way I was leading my life began to haunt me.

"Right after this, I went through a special seminar—a retreat on personal growth. The timing couldn't have been better. It really clicked for me. It said to me loud and clear, 'Stop this nonsense. Stop lying to people. Clear out the garbage! If you don't, you'll never be able to get what you want out of life. You'll just be in this morass forever and these awful things will keep happening to you and you'll keep hurting the people around you.'

"So I did. I decided that many of the guys I attracted were as bad as I was. And the honest ones? I didn't have enough sense to even respect them. So I just stopped lying. I told the truth to everyone I knew, including the men in my life. If I was going out with Peter, I'd tell Paul, 'I'm going out with Peter.'

"A wonderful thing happened. The ones who could take it stayed and the ones who couldn't stayed away. My relationships cleared up wonderfully. I was left with a lot more space in my life for real, true things. It was a good time for me. I got many things sorted out and started to get clear about relationships for the first time. My work was going well. I was in a very good place.

"In addition to being honest, I made two other major changes in my life. The first was that I went out and bought a new wardrobe. I had always been somewhat negligent about the way I dressed, never spending a lot of time or money on clothes. Feeling good about who I was for the first time in a long time led me to want to look good. I guess I felt comfortable projecting a better image once I felt better inside.

"The other thing I did was get a cat. It may sound silly but getting a cat was a big commitment for me. I was a dedicated career woman and getting an animal to care for was a major move. It meant not only having to come home every evening to take care of it, but I also had to arrange for care when I traveled. I got the cat anyway.

"Pumpkin made a difference in my life. Suddenly, there was somebody waiting for me when I got home. Pumpkin was warm and cuddly and . . . slowly I began to become seduced by the comfort of having another creature permanently in my world. Even though I've always loved animals, before I got Pumpkin, I had been reluctant to commit to caring for one. My thinking was, my career simply wouldn't allow it. In retrospect, that was an excuse for fear of commitment. Getting Pumpkin and having the experience be so rewarding started the breakdown of this fear."

Louise's getting a cat is an illustration of the incremental nature of becoming what we value. Imagine, she learned true affection and commitment from a cat. By being able to commit to caring for Pumpkin, Louise demonstrated that she could extend the boundaries of her beliefs about herself and open new doors in her life. She grew used to the concepts of "long-term," "in spite of the difficulty," "care in spite of inconvenience." All this helped her make the mental transition required from fear of commitment to being willing to be committed to a person.

"I met Nick at a training seminar. He was the instructor. The session was out of town and lasted a week. Three days into it, I went shopping after the class was over. I stayed out until the stores closed. It was rainy and I was soaked. I arrived back at my hotel cold, wet and tired. Plus, I had homework to do before the next day's session. I couldn't decide what to do first: take a shower, get some sleep or conquer the work. Then the phone rang. It was Nick asking if I wanted to eat dinner with him. My fatigue vanished instantaneously. I said, 'Of course.' I took a two-minute shower, got dressed quickly and met him in the lobby.

"This was the start of a whirlwind relationship. When the seminar was over, we talked almost every day and saw each other every few weeks. From the beginning, my infatuation for Nick was overwhelming. After about two weeks of intense talking, I realized I was deeply in love. I was in the right emotional place to do this. I had enough time for him. There were no lies. I could be absolutely straightforward and honest with him. I just didn't play any games with him at all. I think that's what was most different about this relationship. I told him exactly what I was thinking and feeling and didn't hedge my bets and didn't hold back. I was a much more honest and open person with him than I had been with anybody in my life. My flat-out openness appealed to him. If I had played any games or done any strange back and forths, like 'I sort of like you, but I don't know . . . ,' it wouldn't have worked.

"It took me 12 weeks to realize that being honest with my feelings about Nick was not enough. The deeper need for honesty was with myself. I had not been lying to Nick but I had been lying to myself. I wanted a permanent partner and a family. As a married man, Nick could not provide this. He was a quality guy, but he wasn't available. That made him not appropriate. I decided that I was too good to be just an affair. I called him up and told him this. I also told him I never wanted to see or hear from him again.

"Later, Nick told me that up until this point he had considered me 'good sex.' He had been married for 15 years, had been having affairs while he traveled for the past four years, and was quite happy with the arrangement. When he received the phone call from me, he was initially angry. Then, as time passed, he began to realize that his feelings for me were deeper than he had acknowledged. He had been leading a double life that wasn't fair to his wife or to me. He sat down and talked with his wife for several days. They both owned up to the fact that their relationship had failed to grow over the years. They had become ossified in the stereotypical roles of wife and husband, which satisfied neither of them. Unbeknownst to me, they decided to terminate their marriage.

"Five weeks after my call, Nick called. He wanted to get together and talk. I refused. He then told me what had happened between him and his wife. We met at the airport. Sitting in the car, he said to me, 'I think we should get married.' I was shocked. I had not prepared for this. The first words out of my mouth were, 'I will make a terrible wife. I don't iron or cook and I'm a terrible housekeeper.' Nick smiled, 'Don't worry. You may be in for some pleasant surprises.' I now know that he is a terrific cook and very talented in a number of areas. At the time, I just accepted his reassurances and said 'yes' on the spot."

Like most marriages, Nick and Louise's has not been untroubled. The major problem they repeatedly faced was the fact that Louise's style was to confront issues head on while Nick preferred to bypass such discomfort as disagreement. He just agreed to whatever Louise desired and then he smoldered underneath. This imbalance cannot be sustained for long before the satisfaction of equal partnership is threatened. Looking back now after 17 years of marriage, Louise and Nick are quick to admit that if their commitment to their relationship had not been a serious one, and if they had not entered marriage counseling after their third year, they would not qualify now as permanent partners.

By giving attention to their relationship, they were able to restructure their marriage into an equal partnership. Nick had been talking "solve your problems" for years. Now he was challenged to live his talk. He readily confesses that he probably would never have been motivated to view Louise as a permanent partner instead of an affair had she not acted as she did. He liked having the comfort of a non-threatening home base combined with the excitement of temporary affairs. He had no desire to change this until Louise forced the issue. Nick, too, had to learn the integrity that comes with living your values. He had to put into practice the values he said he stood for before he and Louise could fully experience the blessings of permanent partnership.

How to Be What You Seek

Change itself takes commitment. When you strike out to improve your ability to "Be What You Seek," it may seem overwhelmingly demanding. Take heart. Learning this step is like learning anything else. Take small steps in a safe environment. Keep practicing until you hit your stride with ease.

For example, if you have been a person who finds "little white lies" convenient, you will probably not experience a metamorphosis into Honest Abe in a day. A place to start is to be conscious of how you act in situations that are conducive to truth-stretching and to plan to correct these first. *Know your tendencies* and just take it one day at a time. Search out the honest people in your life and emulate them. Commit to yourself, "Today I will be as honest as I can be in every situation that comes up. Today I will not tell 'little white lies' for my convenience."

When you allow yourself to be more transparent; when you think, like Pinocchio, your nose will grow longer with every untruth, it is down-right amazing how all of a sudden you begin to realize that you do indeed have power over your thoughts and can monitor your behavior. You can learn to make appropriate choices. For example, it is desirable to be honest and communicate, "I've always wanted children." It is not necessary to say, "I like you except for your big nose." There is such a thing as social grace. What is really important is to focus on what has consequences for your relationship.

When we are unsure about ourselves in relationships we often present ourselves as being less or more than we really are. Pretense drains energy. You will not be happy unless your possible mate falls in love with *you*—not some figment of your imagination or some false front. There is nothing wrong with being yourself. But don't hesitate a moment to *make yourself someone you like being*.

It takes time and energy to implement the principled of "Be What You Seek." But it's worth it. Becoming more whole and becoming more of what you really are feels good. As you keep growing and enriching your possibilities, you will also increase your possibilities of meeting the kind of person you can love and admire. Learn more about who you are by: 1) learning from your projections; and 2) clarifying the qualities you want in others and learning how to manifest them yourself. This process will bring you to more of the wholeness essential for permanent partnership. Take the gamble and give it a try!

Questions and Exercises

Your Projections: For the next week attempt to get in touch with just one of your projections each day. Do this by paying attention when you are upset about someone else's behavior or by what you think they are feeling. When you are aware of this happening, simply ask yourself, "Is it possible that I'm the one who_____?" Just let your answer come. Don't try to deny or force it. Check out with yourself if you feel a little "lighter."

The second week, do your best to be aware of two projections each day. The third week, be aware of three projections a day. Continue looking for three a day until you feel the practice is automatic. As you accept a trait as one of your own, simply look at it, ponder it a moment, and release it. Don't over-analyze it. Just remind yourself that you do indeed have a tendency to do this or that and stay aware. Many times it will give you a laugh. Enjoy it. There's no better form of release.

Qualities You Value: In the previous chapter you clarified for yourself what you really want in a lifelong partner. Now boil it down to the top five qualities that you want most in your mate. What is it that you really value (you did this earlier). Then assess whether or not *you* embody these qualities. You and your partner need not share *all* five qualities but your lists should be close.

Next to each quality that is *not* yet yours but you want to be yours, write down one or more behaviors that you will do for the next week that embodies this value. Do this exercise for six weeks. At the end of this time period, evaluate whether or not you need to continue. Keep going as long as you feel you are developing more wholeness.

For example, if the quality you value is "honesty," here is a sample exercise sheet that shows what this step might look like:

Qualities I Want in Myself	Behavior I Will Demonstrate This Week
1. Honesty	1. I will not give false excuses when I make a mistake.
	2. I will tell anybody who asks my opinion, what I really think.
	3. I will tell the truth when I am asked about my background.
	4. I will not accept a date unless I really want to go.

Now think about *your* commitment to the qualities you value the most:

Qualities I Want in Myself	Behavior I Will Demonstrate This Week
1.	
2.	
3.	
4.	
5.	

Keep working on "Be What You Seek" until you feel satisfied that you "own" the behavior for yourself. Practice does take effort, but remember what your teachers taught you: practice makes perfect.

Chapter 6

How to Be a
Permanent Partner

They can because they think they can.
Virgil

In addition to important steps toward growth through personal relationships, happy partners gave us many insights about how to be a permanent partner. As mentioned earlier, there is much more to lasting love than bells ringing and spines tingling. We are all familiar with the fact that successful people know what they want and set their priorities. Without hesitation, most of us would put our intimate relationships and our jobs solidly on our list of what's most important in life. However, just having priorities isn't enough. We can set our priorities but, on examination, each will have a different sense of urgency. Bottom line, it's the time and energy we put into each of them that counts.

Any priority that doesn't get the time and energy it needs is likely to wither on the vine. It is this sense of urgency that determines what we actually do, what motivates us to give a partnership the nourishment it needs. This fact often escapes us. However, our work, be it at home or downtown, seems more often than not to win the battle of what's really urgent. Several career-minded, over-worked executives have cried on our shoulders when the bad news came that someone else had taken their place with a spouse. Is it that they didn't care about their partners? Not necessarily. The problem is that even though relationships may seem like high priority, they often get relegated to the back burner. Relationships get taken for granted.

Thriving, growing, exciting relationships need tending. We need to apply at least the same sense of urgency to them as we would give to a demanding career or getting our work done in rewarding, successful ways. Relationships demand not only our love but our skills, intentions, determination and *time*. In reality, lasting love without work, devotion, attention and growth rarely happens. Yes, being a permanent partner is indeed very challenging. Even if a relationship is very good, it is not a piece of cake.

Maria: Maria, a bright, witty corporate manager, learned this the hard way. "When I was with the 'wrong' person, the relationship was all work. Mood swings, disappointments, unfulfilled expectations were all tremendously hard work. Unanswerable questions plagued me: 'Am I too affectionate? Perhaps I'm not affectionate enough. Should I say what hurts me or am I complaining too much? If I don't stand up for what's right for me, I'll lose myself. But isn't love giving in sometimes?' Over and over the questions persisted and I thought, 'Surely with the right person, it would be easy. Nothing could be as difficult as these shifts in closeness. Friends one moment and enemies or strangers the next—a roller coaster ride of emotions ending with a pain deep in my very spirit.' I believed that the trick was to meet the 'right' person. The right person and I would mesh so perfectly that we wouldn't even need to use the clutch to shift gears. We would just glide through life's experiences like a marble on polished glass. But when I met Tony and married the 'right' person, I finally realized that believing that a relationship with a partner is effortless—no matter how good the relationship—is just not the truth."

Permanent Partnership Takes Time and Attention

As Maria learned from experience, being successful permanent partners is hard work. But there is a vast difference in the nature and quality of the "work." Working hard at a rewarding partnership is a major attribute of permanency and surely one of the greatest sources of joy. Why? How is it so different? It's different because there is a positive payoff for the work. It's a labor of love. Both partners are committed to building something, to achieving an end result, to deepening the value of being together. Their vision is for a more nurturing, rewarding relationship that is more satisfactory for each partner. They demonstrate their care and concern about the relationship and are not using the situation to act out negative beliefs. Instead, two people put their efforts and energies into making things better for both of them—more pleasure, more warmth, more sense of individual worth and contentment. Even hard times can end up being downright delicious! Who hasn't experienced a *genuine*, "I'm sorry," and melted into forgiveness.

Ted: As Ted, a hard-working, auto mechanic in his early 50's, explains, "I have just as many arguments and rough spots with my wife now as I did in my unhappy, first marriage. But what a difference! Lynn doesn't run away and hide her head in the sand. She hangs in with me and sticks it out until we feel the issue is resolved.

Even though the process can be painful, each encounter seems to deepen our relationship. It feels as if we're pulling the load together instead of each pulling in our own direction, tearing each other apart with no common goal. It also seems to build our confidence that we can work things out, that neither of us is turning our back on the other. We've learned to put great trust in the strength of our relationship. It has taken some time but we both feel now that we can weather the storms. Disagreements, arguments, life's traumas—and we've faced several—won't destroy us."

Permanent partners work to make troubled times, if not smooth, at least less bumpy. The steps you are taking while working through this book will help you with these disjointed times. Finding the compromise position and putting it into action will always be easier if you have the skills, insights and understandings suggested in the Matching Process, and if you temper each encounter with honesty, patience, politeness and love.

Tara also learned that having a partner certainly doesn't herald an end to troubles. No matter how much a couple loves each other and is compatible, life moves on, and much of life is dealing with and solving problems.

Tara and Ken: "Life is full of unpredictable events. Some are bound to cause difficulty. Having a partner doesn't mean an end to bad times. It does mean, however, that you won't be facing life's problems alone. Knowing that my partner is permanent means that as I anticipate the future, I do so with joy in my heart because I know that even though our relationship will have changed, Ken and I will still be together. Together we'll deal with the situations that confront us. If the future is anything like the past, I can look forward to a partnership that is even better, even stronger than it is today. I can't imagine what this will be like because it's so good today. It's a good feeling, though, to anticipate improvement even if I can't imagine exactly how this will occur. Life feels enjoyable now. Knowing that I have a permanent partner by my side makes me optimistic, whereas before I always had this anxious, uneasy feeling about the future."

Commitment and Intimacy

We have mentioned earlier that before a partnership can even begin, we have to deal in some way, at some level of intensity, with the issues of *commitment and intimacy*. There's no doubt that the ability to make a commitment without feeling that one's own soul is lost is essential. We've also mentioned the many ways that we can be programmed not to trust the opposite sex—or our own sex for that matter. In addition, many of us have never seen a "happy marriage" and suffer the void that having no model creates. Or we have bad memories and bad habits from a negative model. And some of us just never want to grow up and take on those awesome responsibilities that go with family.

Society, too, plays a big role. Limited education, limited jobs, limited views of the future inhibit many from the possibility of stable family relationships. For whatever the reason, people who achieve permanent partnership need to overcome any problems they have with making a commitment. They must embrace the idea of commitment to a person, to an idea, to a family, to a set of values. Each couple needs to clarify what commitment really means. We strongly suggest that couples sit down and talk over what commitment means to them before marriage. Ask yourselves, "If commitment is so important to our longevity and happiness as partners, just what does commitment mean and to what is it that we are committing ourselves?" Expectations need to be crystal clear. Boundaries need to be clear. Realities need to be clear. Roles need to be clear.

And then there is *intimacy*. There has been an enduring debate about which is more important in forming personality: heredity or environment? Anyone who has children knows that they all come in quite different packages. Heredity appears to play a very significant role. In fact, one important study was done with identical twins who were separated at birth and raised by different families.[1] After all, identical twins should be the same atom for atom. This research tells us that for most of the traits measured, inheritance was the dominant influence. For instance, a person high in social potency who is a masterful, forceful leader who likes being at the center of attention is very influenced by genes. Traditionalists and those obedient to authority are very genetically influenced. Genes also play a prominent role in shaping a sense of well-being, a zest for life, feelings of alienation, vulnerability, resistance to stress and fearfulness—even a love for the arts. But, and this is a very big and important "but," the one personality trait most influenced by family life is *personal intimacy*. The quality of interaction in a family makes the difference. The more physical and emotional intimacy exhibited by the parents, the more likely this trait will be developed in children. It is natural that people high in this trait have a strong desire for emotionally intense relationships. Those low in this trait will be loners and keep to themselves. When our self-perception and our emotions become distorted in childhood, it cripples us emotionally as adults and makes healthy relationships nearly impossible unless we opt to seek an appropriate cure. However, unlike inherited traits, learned traits can be unlearned and relearned. We strongly suggest that couples considering a partnership, sit down and talk to each other about what intimacy means to each of them. Find out experiences each has had. Find out what each expects of the other. Talk over whether or not both like the same kind of touch, the same kind of closeness.

Acceptance and Trust

Earlier we cautioned: *never marry to change someone*. You would have to tamper either with their genes, their learned distortions or both. In most cases, it doesn't work. You want to be able to fully accept the other just as that person is, not as what your idealized mental image dictates. Acceptance is a precious gift that generates harmony. Good, healthy, intense, dynamic relationships have as their strength the twin pillars of *commitment* and *intimacy*. The underpinnings to these pillars are *acceptance* and *trust*. Unfortunately, when we put all our energies into trying to make someone else a better person, we are often moving the spotlight off our own flaws and refusing to face them. When you accept yourself and become a "better person" *in your own eyes*, you will be more attracted to and admired by people who don't need to be changed. Before taking the plunge, talk over your beliefs and feelings about acceptance and trust. What are your expectations? What are your boundaries?

We all know that many attributes and qualities go into a lasting partnership. Take communication, for example. People must be able to express themselves, to listen fully and to understand each other. Active listening is a profound skill necessary to keeping relationships happy and healthy. These skills alone have filled many books and we urge you to read them. However, our focus here is on what we heard from the successful partners to whom *we* listened. Over and over again, permanent partners told us the same "secrets"—those attributes and qualities that permeated *their* long-lasting, vibrant relationships. We have encapsulated these secrets in the Four P's: 1) Priorities, 2) Philosophy, 3) Peace and personal prosperity, and 4) Passion. These Four P's are a healthy kind of glue that helps partners stick together. Examining them might serve as further clues as to whether or not you are on the right track with a relationship.

Priorities

Permanent partners share priorities. There is no right or wrong answer as to how much time and energy should be devoted to each one, but all the permanent partners interviewed agreed totally on the importance of having the same rank order of priorities. By far, in most cases, they ranked their marriage at the top of the list. A few tempered this stance because of the needs of children with special problems or other unusual circumstances.

A rewarding permanent partnership is a precious gift with which few are blessed and is certainly not to be taken for granted. It is important that issues such as having children, birth control, earning money versus career satisfaction, where to live, who gets educated, how to use family resources, religion, who keeps the floors cleaned and the car serviced, career versus family choices, be made by like-minded partners. While it may be possible to sustain a marriage without basic agreement on these subjects, it certainly makes it difficult. Partners need to share strong feelings about the importance of their marriage compared to other demands on their resources. They must desire a successful union with great passion. If they don't have the requisite skills to make it so, they must acquire them. The following partners explain how they practice shared priorities:

Goldie and Buzz: "I feel so thankful. We've still passionately in love after all these years. We believe the primary reason for our success is that the first priority in both of our lives—the thing that we want more than anything else—is to have a wonderful marriage. It was our number one goal when we started. It still is our number one goal. Children, job, interests are all secondary goals that revolve around our marriage.

"Any great marriage is an evolution. You change your goals, your expectations, yourself, because life doesn't always work out the way you expect. When your marriage is a number one priority, you find that it gives you a reference point for change. You take each change and adapt in ways that enhance the marriage as well as each individual. The end result for me is that I find Buzz every bit as exciting today as when I first met him. When I heard him speak recently at a meeting, I felt freshly snowed by his great way with words and tingled from feeling so much in love.

"The most helpful experience we had in this respect was a weekend seminar called 'Marriage Encounter.' This two-day class taught us, among other things, how to communicate on a feeling level. One of the exercises that they gave us was to write each other a daily letter talking about our feelings. We continued this practice for nine years and we now have boxes of love letters! This required a lot of commitment. But it really paid off. The intimacy that comes out of sharing your feelings on a daily basis is irreplaceable. We learned to communicate on a level most people never approach. There is no holding back in our marriage, no secrets we haven't told. We learned to tell each other who we are and to understand what it feels like to stand in the other's shoes. We listen. Now, when our marriage falls into the doldrums, we start talking about it right away. We have never tolerated our marriage being just okay.

"In 25 years, we have gone to bed maybe three times without resolving an issue. When we've been disagreeing with each other, it sometimes takes tremendous effort to reach across the bed and say, 'Can I hold you?' But one or the other has always managed to do this. By dealing with issues as they come up, they don't escalate.

"There's another thing that has helped our marriage be vibrant— an agreement we made early on. We both feel that we have a responsibility to be grateful and to show it. Out loud! Yes, we say what we love and appreciate about each other out loud. This morning I woke up before Buzz. I stayed in bed until a few minutes before he had to get up. Then I woke him up by kissing him so he didn't have to hear the alarm clock. He looked at me and said, 'I'll never stop loving you. I am grateful for this feeling and happy that you're my wife.'

"Our marriage is a real gift. But, we fought to make it a blessing. It wouldn't have happened if we hadn't made it a number one priority in our lives."

Goldie and Buzz illustrate the axiom that you can *respect* a person with whom you share information but you can *love* a person with whom you share your feelings. But most importantly, every day is a day of creating memories for the next. Happy memories make for happy couples.

Some priorities appear to be more binding than others, and it would be easy to conclude that ranking the marriage number one is a very important decision. But, it seems that agreement on the rank order of priorities is even more important.

Stan and Robin: Stan and Robin have very different personalities. She likes active sports, loves talking with people, and appears extroverted and energetic. She loves her work in a retail store. Stan is methodical, precise and steady as a rock. As a researcher for a chemical company, he spends half his time working alone. They both have children from previous marriages and agree that the children are their first priority.

"We're extremely different personalities but our value systems are the same. We both have children who are still very much in need. Whether they're her kids or my kids, they all have some pretty heavy-duty needs and at times the financial decisions are fairly complex. We both agree that she and I are equal about making decisions that affect our five kids. We both understand that they were our responsibility long before we were responsible to each other. We are each other's primary relationship, but there are times when we need to consider them first. If they need to go to a special school, then we decide together to give up a new sofa, a new car, a new floor, or whatever. We have two kids in expensive, private schools for learning-disabled children. We have one who just graduated from college and one who is on his own but is also very learning-disabled and has lots of needs. When we feel good about the decisions we make, we can pretty well back off from our own needs when we have to. It's very important to be able to do that when you're step-parenting. Kid problems are where your conflicts come in a second marriage. We have very strong feelings, both of us, about being responsible to our children—all of our children."

Concerning agreement on priorities, it is interesting to note that although the overwhelming majority of people interviewed believed their marriage was the most important thing in their lives, devotion to each other did not mean giving up job success. In the long run, organizing the time and energy each spent in the work-place so that there was time and energy for the marriage did not penalize their success at work. On the contrary, it gave them greater balance and stability.

Philosophy

A well thought-out philosophy serves as the best foundation for great marriages. Such a philosophy includes an agreement on what values are important, how they are shared and lived out. While a philosophy of married life may not be verbalized, we think that it's best to talk it over and for some, even to write it down. It's hard to keep unclear contracts. Maria, whom you met earlier in this chapter, illustrates the importance of a common ground.

Maria and Tony: "Early on in my relationship with Tony, he told me that what he wanted in a permanent relationship were three things: honesty, monogamy and satisfactory sex. I was impressed by this, especially since he was serious and wasn't using it as a ploy to introduce sex into our relationship sooner than I felt comfortable about it. I shared his philosophy. I valued his focus and greatly appreciated his verbalization of it. Until he articulated the three components of a successful relationship as he saw them, I had not even thought about them consciously. Now, many years later, I think about them as absolutely essential to our marriage.

"We resolve most of our conflicts by refocusing on these three values. They give security, direction and stability to our marriage. When I was untrusting or jealous early on in our relationship, I would remember the commitment of honesty and reveal to him my suspicions. This was hard for me because I did not want to 'lower' my image by revealing such base insecurity. Having a commitment to be honest helped me win this battle with myself and speak up in spite of being fearful to do so. In response to my questioning, he would remind me of our commitment to monogamy. I would be reassured that nothing would interfere with this promise. Now when I'm insecure, I still remind myself of the three rules. The doubts usually vanish before I feel compelled to verbalize them. We need to go over this baseline periodically and talk about how it's working for us and at the same time renew our commitment to what we value as a team."

Here's what other permanent partners say about the shared philosophy on which they base their marriage.

Patrick and Elayne: Patrick is an outspoken but gentle man who likes structure in his life. Elayne likes to talk thing over and is in high demand for her counseling abilities. "The first month that Elayne and I were married, we developed our philosophy about the way we felt about our objectives in life. If I look at our marriage over the years and analyze why it has succeeded and continues to succeed, it's because we've never deviated from this philosophy. We had a shared value system and this became an anchor in our relationship. Furthermore, we believe that if two of us work at our relationship, we can get more than twice as much out of life.

"The model works like this. Life is an adventure. What you try and do in life is discover your potential. The way we wanted to do this together was threefold: mind, body and soul. We wanted to discover our potential in all three dimensions. All of our energies have been directed not only at becoming better and better in those areas, but also at supporting each other's efforts at improvement. For example, we've done a lot of exercise over the years and still do. In the early years, we jogged together. Now we play tennis and do a lot of hiking. That was the physical part. In regard to the soul component, we worked on our relationships with other people—how we treated them. As for the mind, we clearly shared that. So, the adventure of life became how could we help each improve in each one of these directions.

"Every five years we commit to our game plan; what we are going to do mentally, physically and spiritually. Every six weeks we go to a Bed and Breakfast and take long walks to review our progress. We talk a lot about trade-offs in our lives and in our marriage. In our first three months we established rules that have helped us and that still persist today. The first is the 24-hour rule: if one partner is offended by something the other partner does or says—even if it's irrational, like if she's talking to someone else at a party and I'm jealous—the person has 24 hours to raise the issue or forget it. If it comes up after this, we'll still discuss it, but the other partner doesn't need to feel any guilt.

"Rule number two: One person has no right to force personal values on the other or take advantage of the other. This started out as, 'If you think it's dirty, clean it, or hire someone else,' i.e., if I like a clean house, I should clean it and not expect you to. You can barter all you want, you just don't have a 'right.' We never take each other for granted.

"Rule number three: If you make me a great meal, I have to say 'thank you.' There is an implicit statement that you've done me a favor since I don't have a right to expect this. It sounds strange to say we go around saying to each other, 'thank you, thank you,' but, in fact, we do. You treat each other every bit as respectful and well as you treat a friend.

"Rule Number four: No designated breadwinner. We are equal partners and we discuss all issues. Being fair is important. Also, this means you are always appreciative if your partner does something for you.

"Rule number five: Nobody sits on their ass while somebody else is working, i.e., your work is not more important than the other's. Either we both do something or one of us has a strong urge to do something or we get someone else to do it.

"When we go away we walk and talk about our marriage a lot. Is it growing? In what dimensions is it growing? If it's not, we feel a responsibility to cure it. What are we doing as a couple spiritually? What are we doing physically? How is my individual growth? Am I supporting your growth? When not, why not? What are the trade-offs? Part of looking back at, say, age 60, and asking if you've made the right decisions, is knowing that when you made the decision, you considered the trade-offs. These are important discussions and are the fertilizer of a relationship. The game plan gives us a focus for our marriage, a *raison d'être*."

Ken and Tara: "One of the struggles in a relationship is to decide which set of parents to emulate. We are fortunate that politeness and caring were on both sides. In my case, it was more my mother caring for my father. In Tara's case, it went both ways. Her parents are almost sickening about it.

"Looking out for and nurturing the other person was a major theme in Tara's parents' marriage. It also is an important theme in ours. Things work better when you put the other person on at least equal priority with yourself." Tara interrupts, "The little, silly things that Ken does for me like picking a flower for me on the way back from a walk or opening the car door—real traditional stuff—and my making his cut of meat the better-looking piece . . . feel comfortable as well as special.

"One of the things that was important to our parents that is also important to us is to stay in good shape. Every morning Tara and I get up at 5:30 and go for a run. Sort of associated with this is an unspoken rule that you have to look nice and take good care of yourself and not look like a slob. This helps me. If I were by myself, I would usually be sloppy. Knowing that Tara wouldn't like this helps me be disciplined."

Bob and Wendy: Bob and Wendy are very much alike. They share similar personality styles, likes and dislikes, and love the same activities. Both hold demanding jobs that put constraints on how they use and organize their time. "There are two fundamentals that have helped our marriage be a satisfying partnership. The first is that we both were whole people before we met. We do not look to each other as a source of validation. We each individually enjoy our jobs and our interests apart from each other. We both felt good about ourselves before we were a team. Now, as a team, life is much better, but it's more like having a dessert after a meal, not the meal itself. We were each individually fulfilled before we joined each other.

"The second fundamental that has been useful to us has been to divide up the maintenance portion of our lives. For example, since our jobs are 60 miles apart from each other, we chose to live close to one job and far from the other. The partner that doesn't have the commute—me—has responsibility for the most house maintenance tasks. A carefully thought out, fair division of labor has helped us avoid an area of conflict that some couples experience—especially with children. The entropy that happens in everyday life can kill a marriage!

"We both have the same basic set of values. This makes life together a lot easier than if we didn't. Our attitudes towards our work, life, kids and other people are very similar. We have similar attitudes toward money, for example, so spending decisions are fairly smooth. Our shared interests make vacation decisions easy. We both like to ski, so winter vacations are not hard to make decisions about.

"The fact that we're very much alike has helped our marriage. Even more important than this, however, is the fact that we're both willing to compromise. Even people who share interests as much as we do have areas of disagreement. Both partners being willing to compromise is essential to sustaining a harmonious relationship.

Wendy and I mutually respect each other. In an argument, we try to see the other's point of view. We don't always manage to do this, but we consistently try."

Robin and Stan: "Our relationship started out on a pretty honest basis. It's become a theme we live by. He tells me he tells people this: that he is terribly free to be who he is because I'm so direct and up-front with him, that he can be the same with me. It's a very honest relationship for both of us.

"In order to be a successful permanent partner, you have to respect the other person. He or she may not want what you want or think the way you think, but respecting the other's position is important. Your permanent partner is a person who thinks and bases thoughts upon past experiences and values. Just to respect where they're at is important.

"I am fairly religious and he does not have the same feelings about that I do, but we talked it over long and hard prior to our marriage and made some very firm decisions about how we'd handle that. In fact, we go to church as a result of talking a long, long time and ironing it out in advance. I'm very free to talk about what I feel and what I think without him feeling oppressed. So the value isn't so much the religion; it's allowing each other to have their own beliefs and be okay."

Each of these couples strengthened their partnerships by communicating and negotiating their basic philosophy on making marriage a winning experience for them. They entered into agreements. There are certainly differences in their expectations and desires but they all gave serious thought to their ideals and structured a method of follow-up to keep their ideals in place as much as possible. All of these elements build trust. *If trust in agreements isn't present, all begins to crumble.*

Peace and Prosperity

As a society, we practice war and even have colleges to study and develop war strategies, weaponry, tactics and language. But little attention is paid to what it takes to live in peace. There are very few colleges that focus on strategies for peaceful living. Individual people reflect the problems of the larger culture. We lack the skills and temperament for peace and turn to violence or alienation or settle for peace at any price. We suggest that couples study peace and what goes into allowing it to happen in a relationship. We all need schooling in peace, particularly domestic peace. Police spend 30 percent of their time on domestic violence. Surely there's a better way.

One deep-rooted concern many of us share is that peace can be boring. Conflict is the basis for interesting drama. As you watch a play unfold, conflict is introduced early on. You experience the tension that you hope will be resolved by the end of Act III. Real life is very much the same. We will do almost anything to avoid boredom, including fight. Conflict doesn't have to be of the negative intensity of Who's Afraid of Virginia Wolf, a portrayal of a deeply disturbed relationship, but instead it can be and often is a healthy and realistic part of life. Remember when Marianne gave us her advice for new lovers? "I'd try to find out things like whether this couple has ways of fighting, and whether they know if they get into a fight there's a way of getting out of that fight."

There is little doubt about it, a key to a lasting relationship is the ability to handle conflict in a way that does not devastate either party and that demonstrates trust in the strength of the partnership. You can really love each other, have a wonderful sex life, and laugh a lot, but if you can't handle conflict in a constructive way, the relationship is on shaky ground. People are indeed different. Not only are there sex differences but each person has a unique personality style and a unique set of learned behaviors. It's a miracle that we can get along together at all. A lot of the pain in relationships can be traced to differences that have never been acknowledged, reconciled or resolved.

Interestingly enough, men appear to have a greater problem with conflict resolution in the family than women do. Although we all know of exceptions to this, research does show that women more frequently bring up troubling issues that are causing bad feelings. In contrast, many men tend to withdraw and want the problem to go away. "I don't want to talk about it now," "Why bring up something unpleasant?" and "Okay, I'll just do whatever you say," are common responses to family conflicts. Some men turn to violence, over-reacting in the opposite direction. Training through seminars, books, therapists, or with a good coach officiating at a few arguments are solutions that work for many.[2]

There are definite steps to handling conflict that can make this part of a partnership much more "livable." Learning and committing to this process is best done before the marriage bells peal. But couples interested in a permanent partnership can learn them anytime. As with any "good" fight, it's important to stick to the rules. We've outlined these principles of communication in Appendix E as "Pearls of Wisdom for Conflict Resolution." They are a combination of our experience with interviewees and the known steps for conflict resolution in families. Keep in mind that it takes two determined people to make these skills work well if they are to bring about peaceful solutions to life's everyday problems. Just as Ted and Lynn demonstrated earlier, both partners must agree to this process and, what is even more difficult, be willing to put it in practice when things heat up. The best time to talk over a commitment to conflict resolution is when you are feeling good about each other and in the mood to make your partnership a real winner. A good principle to follow: bring up an issue as soon as possible, inform the other person that you want to have a serious discussion, make an appointment and then carry out your discussion in the spirit of love.

You cannot sustain a lifelong relationship with another human being unless you both dedicate yourselves to ensuring that the relationship grows as you both grow as individuals. This is how a relationship prospers and evolves. The work is twofold: 1) peace—resolving conflict when it arises in a way that strengthens the relationship; and 2) prosperity—seeing that the partnership nurtures the growth of each person, as did Patrick and Elayne. When one partner grows at the expense of another, people eventually move apart. Communication is a key to success in either case. Here is how some couples made it work.

Lisa and Nat: "We're both sticklers for having things clear between us. Nat travels with his job, so this is doubly important. One of the rules in our marriage is never ever leave the house or go to sleep angry. This is quite simplistic, but it's important to us. It sounds so stupid, but if one of us were to go away with an issue unresolved, the thought in the other person's mind is, 'What if he doesn't come back?' I mean, if Nat were to walk out in the midst of an argument and later was killed in an automobile accident, I don't know how I could live with myself. It may seem silly to some, but we always resolve things no matter how tired we are, even if we can only get to the point of saying, 'Honey, I feel okay about this tonight, but we should talk more about it tomorrow.' So, even if we haven't completely resolved it, we know that we still love each other and each person understands how the other feels. It may sound dumb, but this rule has really been important to us considering the fact that Nat is gone so much.

"Another thing that we do is never say anything in front of someone else that would embarrass either one of us. If Nat does something that bugs me, I immediately address it, but I make sure we're alone. Then I say, 'Honey, you hurt my feelings. This is how I feel. Maybe you don't understand it, but this is how I feel anyway.' We have struggled with this and come to the conclusion that it doesn't matter if we agree with each other as long as each understands how the other feels.

"Nat and I are really different in a number of ways. He is more thick-skinned than I am and things bother him a lot less. Therefore, I'm the one who usually feels hurt by an action of his rather than the other way around. When this occurs, we talk and talk until he really understands what I'm saying. Sometimes it takes my repeating my feelings two or three times until he understands, but I can really tell it.

"Another thing we do that I like is that, although it's not unusual for us to disagree, we try hard not to fight. My mother used to raise her voice whenever she disagreed with something. I remember as a child not understanding that my parents loved each other, but their way of communicating was to yell at each other. We avoid this. Sometimes when we communicate it's argumentative, but it's never yelling.

"Compromise is an important part of our marriage. In certain time periods, one of us has done more compromising than the other, but, in the long run, we have compromised an equal amount of time. For example, now that Nat is building this new international business, he has had to give up things in order to spend more time with me. In fact, since his work is so demanding, he has had to give up everything else outside of work in order to have family time. He used to enjoy painting and playing squash. He doesn't do those now because there just isn't enough time. Our major area of compromise seems to be free time. Understanding this and compromising when it counts helps us both feel that we're getting what we want.

"We have an unspoken agreement to help each other. Even when he has worked for many hours, if he comes home and senses I'm exhausted or at my rope's end, he'll do the dishes or take over the baby. He might be tired from working behind a desk all day, but he's not tired from, say, caring for a sick baby, so he relieves me when I need it. We really try hard to be sensitive to what the other person is feeling. That's not easy because you have to get out of your own skin and into someone else's."

Tara and Ken: "One of the problems with our jobs is that at times they consume all of our emotional energy. For example, if I've been traveling or have put in a 12-hour day, I am very edgy. Believe me, sometimes it's very, very difficult to be warm and understanding. I try to be, but the price I pay is sometimes to take it out on anyone called family. Ken understands and allows for this. Likewise, the days that he comes home especially worn out are the ones that I protect him from nuisance items like what's gone wrong with the house.

"The way we resolve conflict has changed a lot over the years. In the first few years of our relationship, we were going through the transition from independence to a partnership. We had to deal with step-kids and kids of our own, and there were some serious struggles. In the beginning, we used to argue when problems arose. Things got very hot and 'tempery' during those first three years. Now, when we get angry, one of us will say, 'We need to sit down and talk.' It used to be Ken who would do this the most. I'm getting better at it. I had a hard time admitting I was wrong and it didn't help when Ken would point this out. Now, when an area of conflict arises, we take a few minutes to get into our little holes and steam and fume, and, in a very short time, one or the other will suggest a rational conversation to straighten out the problem."

Aurora and Sam: Aurora and Sam are a serious-minded couple who run their own business. "Neither of us likes tension in the household or at work. Whenever there is any kind of conflict, both of us seek to resolve it. We choose togetherness as opposed to alienation. Neither likes it when the other is uncomfortable. When we sense a problem, we immediately start working to resolve it. We talk it out. We learned to do this when we were friends working in the same company together. During this time we also learned the importance of letting the other person save face during an argument. If I know that I'm really right and I've backed Sam into a corner, I try to give him an out. What seemed politic in the workplace works just as well with our domestic problems.

"Another thing that we do frequently is to ask forgiveness and make restitution if there has been a tense time. Right in the middle of being unhappy with each other, one of us will make a gesture to relieve the tension and the other person usually quickly recognizes this and drops the subject. We try not to end the day angry with each other. We rarely ever stay angry for more than a few minutes. Sam is very good at letting me know exactly how he feels when he's feeling it. That makes it easy to address issues as they arise instead of burying them until they explode. This makes him easy to be with. The other thing that makes him easy is that he is consistent. He is so consistent that he is predictable. His stable disposition made it easy for me to learn to trust him.

"Sam was very patient with my lack of trust although I realize now, as I look back on our early years, that it must have hurt him because he never gave me any reason not to trust him. My lack of trust had severe ramifications for our marriage. I structured everything when we were first married so as to be prepared for my husband's leaving me. For example, I did not want to have a baby because I was afraid it would make me too vulnerable. How would I take care of a baby if he walked? Sam was very patient with me. His patience plus consistently being there for me, in addition to my working with a therapist, was healing. I gradually came to see that Sam is so stable a man and partner that it was inappropriate to treat him with mistrust.

"Love is something that you practice, not something that you feel. That's what true love is. It's fun to have those wonderful, euphoric feelings and butterflies in your stomach and be infatuated, but that's not love. Yes, love is something that you practice, not something that you feel. You know that your marriage is working if you both feel that you each are doing more than your share."

Passion

Even though permanent partnerships grow and change, one of their characteristics is that they are consistent—not consistent in a way that is boring, but consistent in the sense of being closely aligned and on an even keel. It's like the difference between a ship lost at sea in a thunderstorm and one on course, calmly cruising the ocean. The former is definitely more exciting, but it's not necessarily more desirable.

For permanent partners, the kind of passion that is similar to that felt in the bloom of being "in love" or being with someone new is difficult to sustain. Permanent partners learn to savor and appreciate the steady course. They take control and accept that they have the ability to make decisions about passion every day of their lives. Many couples learned to deepen their skills and appreciation of sexual intimacy. Their self-esteem, their appreciation for their bodies, and their keen sensitivity to the consequences of making love were all important factors. People have different likes and dislikes. Men and women often have different rhythms. Permanent partners care enough to be concerned about the happiness and well-being of each other and don't object to learning about each other's needs. It's like any other skill. Information and practice coupled with caring creates more perfection. For many permanent partners, a satisfying way to ensure passion as part of their partnership is to have "scheduled spontaneity." It may sound contradictory, but sometimes you need to make a "date" with your mate to make sure you have the time, place and energy to be physically close. Our interviewees share their helpful hints.

Goldie and Buzz: "Even though I'd been through a failed, teenage marriage, I didn't know a thing about sex. And neither did Buzz. We both were so Victorian! I thought that sex was something men did that women tolerated. We were young and just weren't very good at it. I only knew what we weren't supposed to do; I didn't know what we were supposed to do. And I certainly didn't think I was supposed to like it! When you're first raising a family and there are babies underfoot, it isn't easy to be passionate. Later, when you have more time and aren't so tired, it's much, much easier. I laugh when I think about this now because it's so different for us today.

"When the children were little, we'd find hotel rooms close to home and escape there for a few hours. We've found that there was a direct proportion between how good our sexual relationship was and the distance from home. Even today when we vacation, we each think of something romantic to bring to the room like candles or incense or whatever. It still is fun and fulfills some of our fantasies.

"Our sex life has gotten progressively more satisfying over the years. The closeness and intimacy that comes from being together a long time may not be as exciting as new love, but it's much more wonderful. It's much deeper, much more deeply wonderful. After 30 years of marriage, I can see Buzz across the room and my stomach still feels jumpy with excitement. Now that's pretty nice."

Lisa and Nat: "How do we keep passion alive? That's a hard one. One thing we do is to plan little trips together. These are our sex, passion trips. We work on them all the time. Otherwise, a month can go by and suddenly you realize that you're missing a vital part of the relationship. You have to have time for sex. Since our lives are pretty busy, we have to carve out a specific night and plan for that to be 'the' evening.

"Spontaneity is wonderful but, practically speaking, waiting until we both have the time and desire would mean waiting too long. If for some reason sex hasn't been satisfying, we'll talk about it. It might have been too fast for me or not strenuous enough for him. We'll say, 'Let's talk about this. What should we do? How can we change this?' From the start, we agreed that neither of us would be coerced to do anything we didn't find pleasurable."

Tara and Ken: "By the end of a weekend, we are feeling wonderful and intimate and romantic. This doesn't last very long during the week because of the very demanding, stressful jobs we have. When you come home from work with a million work problems rumbling around in your head and you have to stop at the market and then after dinner you have to do lunch boxes . . . by the time you get into bed you don't even want to talk. So by the end of the week, we're feeling very 'untogether.' Fridays are frequently 'bomb nights' and sometimes depressing because it's the weekend and you're supposed to be living it up.

"One of the things we do to ensure the nurturing of our relationship is to protect our weekend calendars. We try to avoid making a lot of commitments and attempt to spend a lot of time together. The things that we enjoy doing the most to beat the week of hassles is to withdraw together. We get into the ritual of taking care of each other and doing nice things for each other. We like to run together, read and garden.

"The most exciting night is Saturday night when just the two of us go out for dinner, come back and watch a video, and then have our night of planned spontaneous sex. On Sunday, it's against the rules to invite anyone over for breakfast. This is a slow-moving day for us with long periods of time spent reading the paper and relaxing. By Sunday afternoon, we're feeling as warm and cuddly as we ever do and this lasts until Monday. We used to continue to hope that it would hold out, but now we're resigned to the fact that by Monday evening we're sizzled with the work problems again.

"There's a pattern, a rhythm to our intimacy. We used to spend lots of time on our vacation talking about how we were going to make things better by stretching out the cuddly feelings. We decided to do something like take a walk together every night after dinner just to be away from the house and together with no distractions. The reality is that we're so exhausted normally that we don't do it. All of our plans of ways to hold on to the intimate feelings through the week have never worked. We've now realized that we have chosen lives that are such pressure cookers that we are simply going to do the best we can. We're resigned to the fact that you can't take Hawaii home with you but you can take trips to Hawaii."

Robin and Stan: "I personally believe in going away for three-day weekends so we have alone time. I like to do adventuresome things. If it's different, I'll want to try it. I read through all the articles in a local magazine about all sorts of different activities and look for something I haven't tried before, such as seminars and talks. Also, Stan and I started a group for couples in our age group who are remarried, dealing with the same kinds of things we deal with, stepparenting and so forth. We have those couples that we can do things with. We do a lot of things together without any company. We ask ourselves weekly: What can we do that's different? Where can we go that's not a normal place? We took a trip down the coastal highway recently. We drove very slowly and stopped lots of places and took pictures. We have a book of backroads and, I mean, these are backroads. They're not paved and sometimes have cattle guards; we take unusual kinds of trips like that. Last year we tried season tickets to the opera. This year we got tickets to plays. I think that that's, hopefully, a key to keeping passion alive. You want to add spice and interest to your marriage? Try some different things. The excitement adds to your love-making. And keep on talking and communicating."

Not all couples can afford weekend get-a-ways. But creative couples can think of many ways to carve out personal time together. For example, one couple house-sat for the weekend while friends watched their children. They agreed to an exchange.

Sexual intimacy that satisfies both partners reaffirms a marriage. Permanent partners do their best to nurture the primary relationship and keep it healthy even though it's always in flux.

When you are seriously considering a permanent relationship, put some time and energy into talking over the four P's with your potential partner. Can you agree on your priorities? Develop a common philosophy? Learn skills to accomplish peace and personal prosperity? Discuss ways to keep passion alive in your sexual encounters? If so, you have a winning formula. When you study the couples we interviewed, you begin to see that they have figured out: 1) how to nurture and protect each other in appropriate ways; 2) how to define and solve everyday problems; 3) how to play and have fun together; and 4) how to keep their sex life humming—the four major components of a good relationship outlined in Chapter 4. While achieving all of these elements is a real challenge, the rewards are certainly worth your best effort. What better way is there to invest in yourself than making love grow and last?

We have focused so far on some of the inner changes necessary to become capable of permanent partnership—how to know yourself better, what you want from a healthy relationship, and the steps you can take toward becoming whole. In the next two chapters, the focus moves outward. We encourage you to make a successful search, to make contact with people of integrity in a systematic and safe way. We call it Social Networking.

Questions and Exercises

Ranking Past Relationships: Rank yourself on a scale of one to five as how you see yourself in your past relationships on each of the Four P's. Think of 1 as "very poor" and 5 as "excellent."

Priorities: *1 2 3 4 5*

Philosophy: *1 2 3 4 5*

Peace and Personal Prosperity: *1 2 3 4 5*

Passion: *1 2 3 4 5*

Forming a Strategy: Now study your ranking and circle those qualities that you want to improve. One at a time, develop goals and strategies for yourself to enhance your capabilities. For example, if you have never thought about a philosophy of married life, think about it now and start formulating what seems right for you. Continue thinking about and developing your ideas until you feel satisfied that you have a solid beginning. This could make a big difference in the kind of person who would interest you and also the kind of person you would attract. These are certainly important issues in your search. Be very clear about what permanent partnership means to you. Enjoy the process of crystallizing your thoughts and feelings. Remember that you have a body, a mind, emotions and a soul, and they all need to be respected, nurtured and developed.

Indeed, being a permanent partner is not easy but something special happens when two people commit to helping each other through life's joys, sorrows and rewards.

ENDNOTES

1. Edell, Dean M.D., *The People's Medical Journal*, "Personality . . . Genes vs. Environment," February, 1987, Volume 6.

2. See transcript from "20/20," "How to Fight with Each Other," Nat Stossel, American Broadcasting Company, August 24, 1990. Also, cf Jongeward, Dorothy, *Everybody Wins: Transactional Analysis Applied to Organizations*, Dorothy Jongeward Associates, Walnut Creek, CA, "The Leveling Process (straight talk)," pp. 95-98.

Chapter 7

Step 4: Part 1
Take Charge

Progress always involves risk; you can't steal second base and keep your foot on first.

Frederick Wilcox

In the previous three steps, you have been challenged to take charge of your personal growth and development. When you fully embrace your life, when you do exactly what you love, when you seek emotional and physical health, when you are being complete in your own life and not seeking a partner out of neediness or boredom, when you look realistically at what a lasting marriage takes, you will have accomplished the inner work necessary to make the very best use of Step Four, "Take Charge." Liking yourself more as a person, becoming open, accepting and lovable to yourself, works in mysterious ways. It will help you walk away from relationships which may be destructive. It will help you be both attracted and attractive to the kind of person who speaks to both your mind and heart and also nourishes your soul—the kind of person you've concluded you want to join to enrich life's journey. Even if you are not completely there (and who of us is ever completely finished with personal growth?), you are at least moving along a promising path. The previous steps entail looking inward and doing some heavy-duty soul searching. Step Four is a change in pace.

Now it's time to have some fun.
It's time to start meeting lots of great people.
It's time to be bold and take charge of your social life.

The Random House Dictionary of the English Language lists several definitions of the word "charge":

To fill with the quantity it is fitted to receive;
To suffuse as with emotion;
To supply with a quantity of electricity;
To ascribe responsibility;

To advance by rushing against.

When you take charge of your social life, you will begin:

To fill it as full as you wish;

To suffuse it with enjoyment;

To spice it up with excitement;

To take responsibility for making things happen;

To throw yourself into the adventure of meeting potential mates;

Most of all, to be in control, in charge, at cause.

As you probably are well aware, meeting people of the caliber you want isn't always easy. But that can be changed. In this chapter and the next we introduce you to a new and creative way of having an active social life: "Social Networking." This system is a way to manage your social life on your own terms, a way to put yourself in charge and give up the waiting game. Although the people we interviewed met their spouses in a variety of ways, we recommend Social Networking. Here's how it evolved.

The Birth of the System

Michele, a personnel executive, had been extremely successful in finding key personnel for her company. No matter how specialized the job description, she was able to find just the right person to fill it. Even hard-to-fill jobs rarely took more than three months. Michele often wished that accomplishing her own personal life goals was as easy, as predictable, and only took three months.

One evening, she and a woman co-worker were bemoaning the difficulties of a single-working-woman's social life. They agreed there was little opportunity or time to make high caliber friends, especially of the opposite sex. Also, they felt many possibilities needed to be excluded. Office romances and business contacts often backfired, and Michele's friend didn't want to date anyone in her neighborhood because of a past experience that went sour. In addition, singles' advertisements seemed much too risky. Social events such as those put on by religious institutions were infrequent and often didn't offer enough people with similar interests. Going to bars just didn't feel right and dating clubs were very expensive. In fact, introductions made by friends worked the best, but they didn't happen consistently. None of these approaches tapped into a large group of great men and women who were looking for mates but, for whatever the reason, weren't part of the "singles' scene." How could they get to meet them? They wondered, "Wouldn't it be nice if we could just go out and look for a partner the same way we recruit people for a job?" This provocative discussion created the birthing ground for an idea and Social Networking was born.

Social Networking

Suppose you were recruiting the perfect person for a wonderful job? Executive recruiters diligently and systematically search out the right person for the right job all the time. They don't wait for someone to just walk into their lives with all of the necessary qualifications. They establish criteria. They gather extensive information. They look for a "fit." They know what they are looking for and take charge of going after it.

Social Networking is modeled after the executive search process. We've made appropriate adaptations for a permanent partner search, but the principles are the same. And they really work! Using this approach, you will not only be able to control the number of potential partners you meet, but also how rapidly you meet them. In addition, there is the happy serendipity of increasing your supply of same-sex friends. Isn't that something most of us would like to achieve?

There were a few stumbling blocks to applying executive search methods to mate recruiting. Consequently, Social Network Parties came about as an important adaptation. Everyone likes to eat and many people like dinner parties. Even those who don't like big parties might enjoy a small, select gathering of congenial people and good food all in the comfort of someone's home.

Social Network Parties, then, are small gatherings where people make contact, eat a fine meal together and meet a number of high quality, well-recommended people. Some of the tension typical of a blind date is removed. People recommend their friends for such a gathering and increase the pool for future dinner parties. Also, there is the fun of meeting several people at a time, not just one by one.

Michele and her co-worker set out to test the system. Within a few months they had introductions to well over 300 singles! Every one of them came highly recommended by other high caliber people— people who themselves possessed the attributes of integrity, honesty, intelligence and a genuine concern for others—good people. Within 10 months, both Michele and her co-worker had found permanent partners. Also, by then, many more people than could be accommodated wanted invitations to a Social Network Party. Gatherings organized by other people sprang up not only locally but in many other places across the country. There were even very favorable reports from England and Australia.

How It Works

Executive recruiters' first step in filling a job opening is to get a clear understanding of what the company wants. They study the job description. Beyond that, they ask questions to gain an even deeper understanding of needs. What are the perfect candidate's interests, personality, work habits, style of communication, career aspirations, etc. Of course, the "perfect" candidate seldom exists, but a clear picture is still necessary as a goal, a checklist with which to measure the people who are identified as possible candidates. The same principles of executive search can be applied to a partner search.

You already will have addressed this first task when you complete Step Two: "Know What You Want." With this accomplished, you will recognize a likely potential partner. Then all you will need is for that person to show up in your life. So, let's look at what to do next to make this happen.

Even with extensive files, it is highly unlikely that recruiters would know enough people to instantly fill their job orders. What recruiters do know is *how to search*. So where do they start? They start by approaching all the people they know who resemble in some way the sought-after candidate. Often they call people in the same discipline or similar industry. In other words, they call electrical engineers in a search for electrical engineers or retailers to find retail vice presidents. The important thing to remember is that the recruiter does not care if the people contacted in this first round are available or match the job description. They are not the final candidates. They are the first link in finding the final candidates.

Social Networking, like executive search, works like throwing a pebble into a pond. The ever-increasing circle of waves affects an increasingly wider and wider area of water. The nature of the first wave determines that of successive waves. Therefore, it's important to be selective about the first wave of people contacted.

Whom should you contact? Your first wave should be only people you know, people you like and respect. Quality people tend to associate with other quality people. The more quality people you meet, the more you are likely to meet. As part of the Questions and Exercises, we ask you to create a "quality person list." The people on this list need not be potential partners. In fact, they probably will not be. They will include married people, people already in relationships as well as singles. The only criteria for inclusion in the list is that you know the person to be a good person and of the quality you are interested in as a potential partner. The purpose of the list is to generate the next wave of people—people who are closer to your ideal whom you don't already know. Then that circle of people will create introductions to an even larger circle of people. Eventually, one of these circles will contain your permanent partner.

Because your first wave of contacts includes well-recommended people, chances are those people you meet through them will be of the same caliber. You will do pre-screening before you invite people to a Social Network Party (Questions and Exercises gives you hints for doing this), but it's a good start to let people that you really respect do the initial introductions. They become your quality-search helpers.

The "pebble" executive recruiters use to generate their first wave of candidates is typically a phone call. With Social Networking, we suggest you get things moving with a letter. A very successful letter and accompanying enclosure looks like this:

Letter to Quality-Search Helpers

Dear_____ ,

We are planning a series of gourmet dinners in order to meet some new single men and women. Ideally we would like to develop a circle of single friends who are stimulating, smart, have high integrity and who are genuinely good people. We envision the individuals to be 25 years old or older and to possess a positive, winning attitude toward life.

People who have the qualities outlined above seem hard to find. Therefore, we thought we'd ask our married and single friends who fit this profile themselves to help us in our effort. Would you please spend a few minutes and jot down the names of any people you know who might be appropriate? We will then call them and ask if they would be interested in receiving an invitation to our next dinner. We call these gatherings of quality people Social Network Parties. The only expense to guests is sharing in the actual cost of the gathering such as the cost of a catered dinner or a potluck dish.

An envelope and form are enclosed for your convenience. Leave a blank in any area in which you don't have the information.

Thank you so much for your help. We plan to have a dinner for all "sponsors" like you and share stories about this "project."

With appreciation,

Enclosure to Quality-Search Helpers

To: Date:

From:

These are the people I know you would enjoy meeting:

MEN

_____

Name   Home Phone   Work Phone   Age   Occupation

Comments: _____

_____

Name   Home Phone   Work Phone   Age   Occupation

Comments: _____

_____

Name   Home Phone   Work Phone   Age   Occupation

Comments: _____

_____

WOMEN

_____

Name   Home Phone   Work Phone   Age   Occupation

Comments: _____

_____

Name   Home Phone   Work Phone   Age   Occupation

Comments: _____

_____

You may want to compose your own letter. For instance, you may have different criteria for the kind of people for whom you are looking. But there are elements that always need to be present.

What to Include in Your Letter

1. Specifics about your "ideal candidate." Use the values you identified earlier.

2. Mention that you would like introductions to individuals who are single and that you are interested in recommendations for both men and women.

3. Be specific about what will be required of the invitees. If there is any cost to them, be sure you are candid about it.

4. Explain your reason for sending the letter. Some of the people who receive it may not know you very well and certainly may not have received a letter of this nature before.

5. Make it very easy for information to get back to you. The inclusion of a form to fill out—similar to the one shown—along with a self-addressed, stamped envelope, helps.

6. It's a good idea to thank the people who help. We are strong believers in a fair exchange. An act of appreciation can take many forms. However, if you intend to use a tangible way, include this information in the letter. One way to say "thanks" is to arrange a special "thank-you" event especially for them. But for Michele, Social Networking worked so fast that the thank-you dinner turned into a wedding! This could happen to you.

Organizing a Successful Social Network Party

The dinner parties are an important part of Social Networking. An enjoyable way to both organize your Social Network Party and to implement it, is to team up with one or more friends. Michele initially teamed up with a woman who liked to entertain and who had a very nice, large home. They both treated the project with the same level of seriousness and each worked hard to make it successful. In retrospect, they believe this was key to the team's working as well as it did. Not only could they share the work in contacting people, cooking, and hosting, but they were also able to pool the names of contacts from their initial lists. That way it more than doubled their possibilities. They got so many names for introductions to wonderful men and women that, within three months, they had to computerize the list in order to keep track.

Since there seemed to be so many quality people available to meet, they decided to hold the dinners monthly. The home could accommodate up to 16 people. This required more effort than they felt they were able to spare without quitting their full-time jobs. Out of this came the understanding that it was important to share the work load.

They invited another woman and two men to be part of their core group. Five core members turned out to be the ideal size. This core group was in charge of pre-screening, issuing invitations and organizing food. Core members were easy to recruit. They had work to do, but they also had very special advantages. They were assured of being included in every dinner and were the only ones who had a brief preview of who was coming. In fact, the members of the core group were the only people who were invited to every Social Network Party. Everyone else was new. This put participants on the same footing, but the organizers got the opportunity to meet new people from all the groups they hosted. The organizers encouraged individuals who wished to get to know each other better to meet outside of the Social Networking structure as their follow-up.

If you plan to team up with one or more people, make sure everyone has the same level of commitment and is willing to devote the required time and effort to making it successful. The dinners become progressively easier to hold, but the first few can be time-consuming to get underway because you want to be absolutely certain that you build a reputation for great gatherings. Your first few will establish this if you thoroughly pre-screen invitees to be sure they are the kinds of people you wish not only to meet yourself but to introduce to other fine people.

Try hard to call every person who is recommended to verify the information given and to ask if they would be interested in receiving an invitation. Don't offer or promise an invitation during this first phone contact. Simply attempt to determine if the individual is a likely candidate to receive one. In Michele's experience, the list was so long they never actually called everyone on it. After the first 30 people, they felt that they had more than enough from whom to choose. You will find hints for successful pre-screening in the Questions and Exercises at the end of this chapter.

Social Network Parties do cost money. At the beginning, the organizers felt that, until they were sure they were providing something of value to the people invited, they should bear the costs and the work ourselves. The fledgling two-person team paid for the first two parties in addition to doing all the cooking. They soon learned this was not at all necessary. These parties were so successful that the next one was done on a potluck basis. Finally, they ended up having them catered and charging the invitees the cost of the catering. By this time, word had spread about these wonderful gatherings, and they started getting spontaneous calls asking for invitations. Not one person objected to helping shoulder the financial burden.

Sixteen people were invited to the first gathering. This turned out to be an optimum number from which the organizers rarely deviated. A group this size is intimate enough so that everyone meets everyone else and yet large enough so there is a selection of people. Also, it lends itself well to two tables of eight people. Later, when they became highly desirable events, many invitees offered their homes as a setting. Even for a very special Social Network Party that was held in a rented mansion able to accommodate a large number of people, they still ended up inviting no more than 16 people. Groups larger than this could become unwieldy, with too many people to ensure that everyone enjoys the get-together. What makes these gathering so successful is that everyone has a chance to meet and talk with everyone else. Since it is unrealistic for most homes to accommodate 16 people, don't let that number stop you. You must decide what would work in the space available to you. However, if at all possible, try to have at least eight.

Here's a description of the first Social Network Party. "We started off with something to drink and hors d'oeuvres. That gave people a chance to mingle. Next a meal was served. We used two tables in two separate rooms. Half the people were in an eating area in the kitchen, the others in the dining room. This had the effect of creating two smaller groups which made it easier to meet everyone at the tables. Place cards indicating where people were to sit were at each table-setting. On the back of the place cards were names indicating where people were to sit for dessert. In between dinner and dessert, the men moved to the other table while the women remained seated. Either way works fine. Consequently, by the end of the meal, each person had talked to new people, half being of the opposite sex. By the end of dessert and coffee, they had met the others."

At first, the organizers gained feedback by phoning attendees and talking to them about their evening. This was very time-consuming. Later, it was changed to asking the participants at the end of the evening three things: 1) a discussion of how the evening had gone and suggestions for future improvements; 2) recommendations for future settings and types of gatherings; and 3) recommendations for other people to be invited to such an affair. They provided a pad of paper with a pen for people to jot down names and contact information and also a stack of forms with self-addressed envelopes similar to those sent out with the original mailing. This discussion turned out to be a great way to end the event. People had one more opportunity to see each other, hear each other and get further acquainted.

To end with a group activity in which everyone participates is a way of ensuring that the event has a sense of closure and that everyone feels included. It not only allows everyone to experience all the others in the group, it also provides valuable information on ways to improve the dinner parties. The decisions to rotate houses, do the meals potluck and ultimately catered, all grew out of suggestions made by participants. When you are ready to give your first dinner, planning ahead helps.

Helpful Hints for Your First Social Network Party

1. Spend as much time and energy as required to ensure your first dinner is successful. Talk to every person on the phone. Gather as much information as possible, then try to match the list of invitees so there is similarity in age but diversity in occupation. It is too easy to talk "shop" if you have more than two people in the same occupation.

2. If you can, hire people to help with the actual event. For the original Social Networking Party three teenagers were hired to pass hors d'oeuvres, serve the meal and clean up. They made it easier for the organizers to socialize and weren't too expensive.

3. Make sure that everyone meets everyone else. This is most easily accomplished by planning ahead and organizing suitable ice breakers rather than by relying on a host or hostess to introduce everybody. For example, using place cards to indicate seating arrangements and then switching seats after the main course is a good way to encourage people to talk to several other people. Other ways to accomplish this could be through the use of party games which encourage the exchange of information, or ice breakers such as name tags. One group played a modified round of charades; guests guessed each person's occupation. Another group did the same to guess each person's favorite pastime. Mixers that are fun and don't embarrass anyone are a good strategy.

4. Concentrate on making your Social Network Party an overall success and do not focus on trying to match the picture you have in your head of your desired permanent partner. In other words, do not read the descriptions you get of people and decide on inviting only those in whom you would be personally interested.

One party did not succeed because the host invited several more women than men and deliberately included men he considered "duds" so he wouldn't have any competition. Well, he didn't, but people were reluctant to come to his second dinner and there never was a third.

Attempt to get a balance and mix of people. Think long term. Probably your permanent partner will not be among those invited to your first event. The primary goal is to have a successful gathering for everyone. Everyone should have an enjoyable time and refer others who will in turn refer others. Michele met her permanent partner on her third event. A woman she had only talked to twice who was a person of high integrity gave her the name of a person who in turn referred her to her permanent partner. Michele almost didn't send her a letter because they were not close friends. Another core member met her match at Social Network Party number 19. Be patient.

5. Limit the size of your core group to two or three people for the first two or three affairs. It is more work this way, but it is easier to control the quality of the events. Later on it helps to have a larger core group. If you can host as many as 16 people at a time, a core of five is ideal. Smaller gatherings suitable for most homes can be accomplished with a smaller core. But, in the beginning, keep it manageable. Do what you can to enjoy the process while anticipating the results. After all, life is a process—not a goal.

6. Create your own kind of get-together. It can be as formal or informal as you wish. We know about barbecues, bowling parties, brunches. One enterprising young man organized midnight feasts. He was a "night" person and wanted to meet like-minded people. Another person loved the opera, so his dinners included a request that participants bring a piece from their favorite opera recordings. A woman in Boston held mystery parties. A retired tennis pro held tennis parties. Social Network Parties can be simple, elaborate, costume, black tie or come-as-you-are. They are a great opportunity to be creative.

However you choose to do it, Social Networking—contacting people you know and admire for names of people they recommend for a singles' gathering, contacting those recommended, and organizing a comfortable place for them to get acquainted—gives you a wonderful way to take charge of your social life. The next chapter will give you even more ways to improve your search. As one successful party-giver enthusiastically claimed, "In spite of the work they entailed, they were a lot of fun. We've made a quantum leap in our social lives and we now feel in control of a social life that before had controlled us. We also definitely expanded our network of the kind of friends we've always wanted to have." When you have taken the previous steps and are prepared to meet your permanent partner, Social Networking will introduce you to as many quality potential partners as you wish—and to some new, good friends. Don't wait to be discovered. Take charge! Plan some fun in your life. Create and enlarge your circle of wonderful friends. You can't lose.

Questions and Exercises

These suggestions are to help you get started on putting Social Networking to work for you.

Find Your Quality-Search Helpers: Find a quiet place where you can focus your thinking and memory. You need to create two lists. The first will have all the quality people you currently know—people you respect and admire. The second will have all the quality people you used to know but may not be in contact with right now. Think back to grade school and high school. Remember the neighbors you had when you were growing up. Think about friends you made in summer camp or in the armed service. You want your lists to be as comprehensive as possible so include people of all ages. Include people that these people know who may also be able to make referrals. Include anyone you respect, i.e., your doctor, attorney, next-door neighbor, barber. Some day a person on these lists could refer you to your future permanent partner or at least be an important step. Don't let shyness or embarrassment stop you from your search. Remember that these lists are not intended as lists of possible permanent partners. They are people who will participate in your search by *recommending* possible partners. The only requirement is the people themselves have characteristics you admire, such as honestly, integrity and a caring nature. Review your lists several times to make sure they are complete.

Quality people I currently know:

Quality people I used to know:

Your Contract: When you have a feeling that you are ready to try a Social Network Party, make a contract with yourself. Write out your intentions. Then set a time frame for each step. And remember, contracts can be re-negotiated but they shouldn't be broken.

My intentions _____

I will contact a core group by (date)_____

We will have our list of people to help with
    referrals by (date) _____

We will have our list of potential "invitees" by (date) _____

Our target date for our first dinner will be _____

Signed _____ Date _____

Pre-Screening Hints: These hints are for screening potential invitees for your Social Network Party.

Opening Statements: Since you will be talking to someone you don't know, you will want to say who you are, why you are calling, and establish whom you know in common to give your call legitimacy. For example, ask, "Is this _____ ?" Then tell them the name of the person who referred you and say, " _____ suggested I call you. I am organizing a dinner for potentially compatible singles to meet each other. We call such gatherings Social Network Parties and they will be _____ . " Explain the kind of social affair you are planning such a catered dinner, mystery party, barbecue, etc. Then, "I want to check to see if you would be interested in receiving an invitation."

Second Statement: If the person shows interest, you want to offer some information and gather a lot of information. The best way to do this is to intersperse the two. First, give some information in the second statement and then ask for some in the third. For example, "A friend and I decided we want to expand our network of friends who are likely to be compatible and who have certain qualities such as personal integrity, honesty and concern for others. We decided to host some parties where such quality men and women could get together in a comfortable and pleasant setting. _____ (your quality-search helper) suggested you might be interested in attending. Your cost would be $_____ for a catered dinner." (If anything is required of the person, state what this is, i.e., potluck dish, cost of cleaning up, costume, etc.) Do you think this is something that would interest you?

Third Statement: You want to confirm the information you have on this person and get some additional information. Start with an easy, straight-forward question first, such as confirming address, job classification and marital status. Save questions which might be considered awkward for later. For example, "I would first like to confirm what I already know about you and fill in some of the things I don't. You live at _____ (their address), you are a _____ (occupation), and you are single. Is this correct? What else can you tell me about yourself?" At this point, the person might need some prompting and may ask something like "What do you need to know?" Answer: "Whatever you think is important for me to know so that we can include you in a dinner party with people we think you might enjoy."

Final Statement: You want to conclude the phone conversation after you have a feel for the person. Does the person sound congenial, companionable, intelligent? Is the person outgoing or shy? (Some of each makes for a good mix at a social gathering.) You also want to give this person a chance to ask questions so that if you decide to send an invitation, he or she will be motivated to attend. You want to sell your Social Network Party at this stage to anyone who seems a likely candidate for an invitation. But don't promise anything that won't materialize. For example, "Well, I have asked a lot of questions so far. It's your turn. Is there anything you would like to know about this dinner?" Then answer the questions.

You want to set the stage so the person won't feel singled out for rejection if not invited. Close with something like, "We have a Social Network Party every month or so and try to invite a new group of people each time who would enjoy knowing one another. I cannot tell you when you will receive an invitation because they fill up quickly. Also, since there are several of us calling to invite people, I do not know how many people have been invited to the next one. But I have enjoyed talking with you and hope I get a chance to meet you someday. Good-bye for now and thanks."

Does this sound like something you can do?

If not, what adaptations can you make to feel more comfortable?

Remember you can share this responsibility with other core group members, and it is a critical step to having the kind of people you want to have as a circle of friends. So don't be shy. This could be the start of something really special in your life!

Social Network Party Guide

What is the kind of dinner get-together you like best?

How can you adapt your first event to suit your tastes?

Do you know a couple of other people who have similar tastes?

Could they be your core group?

If so, when will you contact them?

When you are on your way and get to the actual dinner stage, you are in for a real treat. If you have done your homework, your search and your pre-screening well, you are going to meet some dynamite people who should add a whole new dimension to your life.

Chapter 8

Step 4: Part 2
Create More Possibilities

Chance favors the prepared mind.
Louis Pasteur

There is no question about it. Social Networking works. If you feel competent in the previous steps and if you only need an introduction to your permanent partner, there is no more efficient, practical, cost-effective method to leave the single life behind. The reason this system is far superior to other methods is because it gives you control and selectivity. *You* determine who gets included. You are not dealing with a sea of unknowns. If you have done your pre-screening calls well, you can be fairly certain that everyone who attends a dinner will be the kind of person you would like to know, regardless of whether or not everyone is an optimal, permanent-partner candidate. Plus, because of your pre-screening, you get to know some details about all of the attendees before you actually meet them. This allows you to skip many boring opening lines such as, "What kind of work do you do?"

There are at least two other very good reasons why Social Networking is the best method:

1. It attracts a population of people who are hard to access otherwise. For example, a large number of newly divorced or widowed people are reluctant to enter the "singles" world. Many of these are high-quality people who feel uncomfortable attending large gatherings or functions which are labeled "singles" with people they don't know. It's just too big a transition from the lives they are used to leading. However, a Social Network Party is different. It is more comfortable going to someone's home for dinner than it might be to attend a function such as a singles' dance. It's a safe way to start the journey of learning how to socialize in a singles' world again which is no easy accomplishment.

2. When you are the organizer of a Social Network Party, you determine the timing and the frequency of the events, plus you are assured of being invited to every one. So, you are in charge of

how slowly or rapidly you meet potential partners. Attendees are not so fortunate. In fact, one of the only complaints we've heard is from participants who had a wonderful time and wanted more invitations. It is not customary to invite people back. This, of course, has nothing to do with who they are but with the fact that the purpose of such an event is to meet *new* people. Previous participants should be encouraged and helped to organize their own parties if they want to continue to expand their sphere of friends.

As a serendipitous consequence, the core group of the first dinner found that word quickly got around about what great people could be met through Social Networking and the hosts became mini-celebrities. As a result, they received invitations to far more parties hosted by others than they could possibly attend.

When all is said and done, the main reasons we believe Social Networking is superior to other methods of meeting suitable singles are: when you are an organizer, you ensure quality control by controlling the timing, who is present and the nature of the experience. Social Network Parties provide a safe and pleasant experience in which congenial people can gather and get acquainted.

Creative Variations

As you already know, we recommend Social Networking as the all-around, most effective way to meet the kind of people you want to meet, and for good reasons. However, as interested singles learn about the method, certain reservations sometimes surface. As a consequence, to stimulate your creativity, we'd like to tell you about some possible options. We've put this section in a question-and-answer format to facilitate finding responses to concerns you might have. Skip what doesn't interest you.

Q. *I like Steps One through Three of the Matching Process but I don't think I can do Step Four because I just don't like "parties."*

A. There are actually three parts to Step Four. The first is an inventory of all the highly regarded people you know who might know of quality singles for you to meet—your quality-search helpers. Second, you need a pre-screening mechanism to determine whether or not the people referred to you by them are indeed people who are both qualified and interested in meeting others. You can definitely proceed with these first two stages even if you don't like dinner parties.

The third part of this system is the actual social gathering itself. The Social Network Party functions not only as the means for you to meet all the referees but also as an incentive for your "helpers" to give you introductions to their friends and acquaintances in the first place. In other words, someone receiving a request in the mail to provide an introduction to their single friends is more likely to do so if they feel that the friends they are referring will gain something (like an invitation to dinner) with little risk. Therefore, we recommend highly that you offer some type of organized activity. It doesn't have to be a meal or a "party." However, you should offer a group activity where people have an opportunity to talk to each other, i.e., a tennis match, bowling competition, picnic on the beach, trail hike, etc. This is an extremely important component of Social Networking.

If you really hate groups and such alternatives won't work for you, then, by all means, adapt the method accordingly. When you write to your search-helpers asking for referrals, you might ask directly for introductions for yourself. In effect, you are asking your friends to play matchmaker for you. Lots of people in our study met through their friends doing just that.

Q. *I am embarrassed to write to people I know, especially people in a business setting (didn't you suggest including doctors, lawyers, dentists, accountants, bosses and the like?) some of whom don't even know I am single. Won't they think I am "weird" or "pushy"?*

A. Let's face it. Some people *might* think all kinds of negative things about your approaching them for help. But, experience shows that both in executive recruiting and in Social Networking the vast majority of people feel flattered to be approached and delighted to participate. Most people want to be helpful. Some may even be holding back from making suggestions to you because of their fear that you may think *them* pushy or meddling.

Remember that Michele met her permanent partner because she sent a letter to someone she knew professionally but not personally. Yes, at first, she was a little embarrassed to admit she wanted introductions to other singles. In fact, Michele's embarrassment almost stopped her from sending the letter. But, luckily, she decided to take a chance and send the letter anyway. Not only did this person end up referring the man who became Michele's husband, but she thought the Social Networking idea was so unique, she told friends in England about it. Thus the first international Social Network Party was born. When you toss the pebble in the waters, it's amazing what ripples happen.

Q. *I think the idea of meeting other singles in a pre-screened environment is a good one, but why bother to go to all that work? Why not just fill your calendar with singles' events?*

A. Going to events sponsored exclusively for singles is a good way to meet like-minded individuals and we encourage you to do this. However, these events are not always available in some areas. In the places where they are, they are not always available at optimum times. We do offer one caution, however. At a singles' dance, dating service, or even a church group, *anyone* can attend. One woman in our study met a good-looking, seemingly successful man through a dating service whom she later discovered had served time in prison for child abuse. This service supposedly did extensive pre-screening of its members. We would like to believe that a person with this type of history would not be referred by someone you know and highly regard. Therefore, be selective about what other singles' events you attend. Make sure you do a thorough job in checking the credentials of those who are doing the selecting for you.

Q. *I liked your approach to meeting a permanent partner until I came to the description of the first dinner you organized. I hate to cook. I hate giving dinners. How do I get around this?*

A. You need not empty your oven of the canned goods you've stashed there or clear away the plants which live in your kitchen sink. You can organize a Social Network Party by having one which is potluck (call it a gourmet dinner if your crowd doesn't like the sound of potluck). To add some interest, give your gathering a theme. Call it a Mexican Fiesta or a New England Boiled Dinner (this is for especially brave people), or an Hawaiian Luau. If these ideas don't suit you, consider hiring a caterer and charging the cost of the meal to the participants.

You can even hold your dinner in a restaurant. If you choose this route, we suggest limiting the participants to eight. Tables larger than eight are difficult to find at a restaurant. Plus, it's unwieldy to talk to the people at the other end of a table that seats more than eight. What happens is that you end up conversing primarily with the people seated nearest you. If possible, find a restaurant that offers a private room or, at least, some space designated for your group which isn't surrounded by other dinner guests. One very good dinner party was held buffet-style in a Chinese restaurant which offered a private room that accommodated a large group of people. Each wave of servings, i.e., hors d'oeuvres and soups, entrées, desserts, was accompanied by a shift in the seating arrangements. After dinner, people lingered over tea and milled around for almost an hour before gathering in a final meeting. This more private setting would have easily accommodated up to 16 people.

It is true that holding a Social Network Party in a restaurant means you will lose some control over how the evening goes. Also, in our experience, it's often harder to create a relaxed atmosphere sitting down in a restaurant with a group of strangers than it is in someone's living room. Even though there are some drawbacks, by all means try it this way if you really hate to cook and can't find a core group member who feels differently. Get creative about ways to save yourself the cooking, but always do your best to create an atmosphere suitable to the situation and its purpose.

Q. *I don't want to invite people I don't know into my home. I think it is dangerous, and besides, I don't have a place nice enough to host a dinner party.*

A. The security issue is always one to consider. That's why we suggest you only get names from search-helpers whom you know to be people of integrity who would only recommend people of integrity. The security issue also reinforces the need to maintain as much quality control as you can. If this issue really disturbs you, try using a neutral facility. An obvious one, of course, is a restaurant. See our response above for tips on entertaining in a restaurant. There are certainly other options. Many organizations have rooms for public use. One man met his permanent partner at a Social Network Party held in a church recreation room. Another successfully used a social club to which he belonged. Social Network Parties can be held at places like the Y.M.C.A.s, synagogues, swim clubs, parks, condo clubrooms, beaches, and the like. Get creative about the possibilities. They are endless. You only need two elements: a kitchen (if needed) and a space large enough to hold the tables and chairs to accommodate your gathering. We highly recommend that you check out such rooms carefully and make sure that you can create the kind of ambiance you feel is suitable.

If your concerns center primarily around the issue of your not having a home spacious or nice enough, start thinking about other people's homes. You may want to search out a core member who has the type of home you need. Also, after your first party, you can solicit donations of other people's homes. This was very successful in the past. There were many, many offers.

Q. *Where are all the great women? Everyone I meet is either desperate to get married before we've had our second date or else is such a super-*

woman that I don't fit into her life? Why bother with a Social Network Party? I'll just meet more of the same.

Or,

I was married for 15 years and have been divorced for eight years. Before I married, there seemed to be all kinds of great men around. Since I've been single, I don't know where all the nice men have gone. I haven't met any. So what use is a Social Network Party?

A. We feel that Social Networking helps to address these common problems. By their very nature, the Social Network Parties tap into a select group of people whom you just don't meet otherwise, people who have been personally recommended by people whom you already regard as high caliber individuals. Because of that fact, they are people you, too, are likely to enjoy knowing.

As we get older, the people around us who are single may not seem as desirable for a variety of reasons. The problem is complex but we need to look at two issues. 1) The problem could be our own. Deep down we are not ready for commitment. Consequently, we continue to fool ourselves that *we* are ready but find fault with everyone else. It's a tough one to face but we need to ask, "Could it possibly be true?" Ask, "Am I really ready to give up the single life?" 2) In contrast to such a personal issue, the problem may be that we have not found the right group of people to develop as friends. Several singles told us they had even given up looking for a mate because everyone they met seemed severely impaired emotionally. This led them to drop out of socializing altogether. Others despaired of ever finding the right person, so they settled for relationships which were unsatisfying. Or, they repeatedly had quick encounters with anyone they met who seemed available. Unhappiness was their payoff.

Meanwhile, great people—real potential permanent partners—were right around them all the time. They lived down the block, worked in the same building, vacationed in the same places, went to the same doctor, etc. They just never got to meet them. Enlist your trusted acquaintances to introduce you to such people. First, ensure that you are not relationsick so you can recognize winners when you see them. Then it's only a matter of time before you feel differently and, instead of despairing, are impressed by the number of wonderful potential partners all around you.

Q. *Social Network Parties are too much work! I have a full-time job which leaves me exhausted at the end of the day and, sometimes, I have to work overtime. When do you expect me to find the time to make up "lists," write letters, call people to pre-screen them and then host a dinner?*

A. You're right. Social Networking requires work. Even if you follow our recommendation and team up with one or two other people to help carry the load, they are still work. There is no getting around it. In order for this method to be successful, you need to be ready to make a significant investment of time and effort. However, take heart. After your first one, *subsequent ones get easier and easier.* Keep in mind why you are investing time and effort. It is worth it! And besides, if you are like most people, searching for a mate is a time-consuming activity no matter what methods you use. Think about how much wasted time you already spend looking. At least with Social Networking you have a good chance of meeting a group of companionable single men and women as potential friends with the added possibility of finding your permanent partner.

Q. *I am in my 50's and I grew up in an era when "nice girls" did not call "fellows" up on the phone and invite them out. I know that times have changed, but I feel awkward doing the pre-screening calls you recommend.*

Or,

I feel like a teenager calling women up for dates. It somehow seems belittling.

A. We see two possible solutions. Either get help or learn to try something new. Why not find someone to work with and ask your team member(s) to handle this portion of the method? There are always people who really like talking on the phone. Or, why not try to make the calls yourself even if the idea seems uncomfortable to you right now? Keep in mind that you are not asking someone out. You are merely calling someone to whom you have an introduction to find out whether he or she would be an appropriate candidate and interested in an invitation. There's a big advantage to actually hearing a person's voice and manner on the phone. Any subsequent invitations can be in written form if you feel uncomfortable delivering them verbally. Also, some people take comfort in the knowledge that when they are making pre-screening calls, they are calling individuals of *both sexes.* This somehow takes the "heat" out of the feeling they are calling a member of the opposite sex to ask them out, which, of course, is not what the initial phone call is all about. Proper screening is critical if you want your Social Network Party to be a rousing success.

Q. *I have terrible fears that when I invite people to a Social Network Party, no one will want to come.*

A. In the worst possible scenario, this could be true, but we don't think so. It is common to have fears about things we haven't done before. However, you need to get at what makes you so scared. Do you suffer from low self-esteem, lack of readiness? If so, we recommend you invest more time and work on the first three steps: "Heal Any Wounds," "Know What You Want," and "Be What You Seek." Remember that one of the symptoms of low-self esteem is a deep belief that you don't deserve to be loved. When you love and respect yourself, you become more lovable. Ungrounded fears of rejection melt away.

Also consider that maybe there is something in the way you handle or project yourself which makes it difficult for people to approach you. This was the case of one man who put people off because of a brusque sound in his voice that he wasn't even aware he made. When you got to know him, this didn't make as much difference. He had to ask trusted friends for their feedback. So did a woman who, even though she was 42 years old, sounded as if she were ten on the phone. Once we open up our blind spots and become aware of previously unknown habits, we can usually alter our behavior in a more satisfactory direction. Trusted friends, if their honesty is encouraged and accepted, are often the best way to get feedback about how we come across to others. However, if the problems go deeper than those with which friends can deal, don't hesitate to take an Extra-Strength Dose cure. See a qualified professional for assistance.

Experience tells us that others will be delighted to attend your Social Network Parties. Your best "fear insurance" against rejection is to have done a good job of pre-screening and to offer an invitation only to the kind and quality of people you really want to know. They, too, are likely to be interested in meeting congenial people. Remember, there will be several people other than yourself at your dinner who will all contribute to its great success. This is not like being on a blind date where the risks are much higher.

Q. *I don't know more than a handful of quality people to whom I can write my initial letter. Since I doubt this will give me a large enough pool, what should I do?*

A. You are right. Five or six people is not a big enough pool. Try to come up with closer to 10 or 15; more would even be better. Are you sure your list is comprehensive? Did you include people of all ages and marital status? How about asking the people of integrity *you* know to give you names of people they know who could give you good referrals? Think hard so that you haven't left out significant people. Be creative about your list but don't lower your standards.

Remember you probably will be teaming up with one or two other people. Look for people who perhaps have a wider circle of friends than you do. They will not only make their own contributions but may also jog your memory, triggering options for possible search-helpers you had forgotten. Select your team of contributing friends carefully. They will probably be your core group.

Here are four stories that illustrate reservations and the use of creative options.

Emily: Emily is a petite, gracious woman who works as a clerk typist. Two and half years ago, just before her 54th birthday, her husband suddenly died. Emily had been married for 32 years. The thought of the possibility of being single for the rest of her life did not truly register until she had been a widow for over a year. As the shock of being widowed was replaced by loneliness, Emily realized that she was being excluded from many of the social events to which she had been routinely invited when she was married. It's not that her friends deserted her entirely, it's just that suddenly she didn't quite fit with the couples who had comprised her social sphere up until her husband's death. Yet, she didn't feel "single" either. When one of her best friends volunteered to set Emily up with a cousin of hers, Emily didn't know which was worse: the feeling of betrayal to her husband or the sense of incompetence and fear because she didn't know the first thing about dating. Another of her friends had heard about Social Networking and suggested she try it. Emily cringed at the thought. "I'm just not ready. I feel panic just at the mention of it. And besides, I can't afford to invite a group of people to dinner. I'm barely able to make do feeding myself."

A year later, there had been some changes in Emily's life. She had joined a bereavement group of widows and widowers and, although still in mourning, she felt ready to meet other single people. She explains, "At the time, I needed single women as well as men friends. My old group of married friends were all couples and even though we liked each other, we had begun to have different interests. Besides, my widowhood had left me financially devastated. I knew they still accepted me, but being with my old friends just didn't feel comfortable anymore."

Emily remembered Social Networking and decided to put it into action. She approached a woman and a man in her bereavement group and suggested they operate as a team. The woman volunteered her home and the man took care of the mailing costs. All three contributed names of quality friends who could become their search-helpers. The Social Network Parties they organized were all potluck.

To make them a little unusual, they varied the food theme of each, starting with an Italian dinner and then a Mexican dinner.

Emily made several good friends among the women she met and her permanent partner appeared at her eighth Social Network Party. He was a 52-year-old man who had been divorced for 13 years. Dinner that night was to be country American and he volunteered to bring a home-baked apple pie. "I knew he was a sweetheart from the first," she said with a twinkle in her eye, "and boy, can he cook!"

Ryan: Ryan hates parties. He is a private, soft-spoken person, and somehow the idea of attending any kind of a party did not appeal to him. When he was separated from his wife of 22 years, a friend suggested Social Networking but Ryan refused. "However, certain parts of the method appealed to me," he now admits. " I always believed that the first step in achieving a goal is to define the goal. If this works in business, why not in a personal situation? So, I sat down and wrote out a list of qualities of an ideal wife for me. I wanted someone smart and compassionate who had been married before. Physical looks didn't matter so much, but I didn't want someone a lot older than I am because I also wanted to have children. So age and desire for a family were also on the list.

"Then, I sat down and thought about who would know someone who would fit my list. I just didn't feel like approaching everyone I know and admitting that I wanted to get married again. After all, some people didn't even know I had gone through a divorce. So, after thinking about everyone I knew who could help find someone, I settled on the wife of one of my basketball buddies. I didn't know her extremely well, but she was an outgoing, friendly person who seemed to have a good head on her shoulders and I knew she and my buddy had a good marriage. I asked for her help and she immediately went into action. She gave me a list of women she considered suitable.

"I called the first woman on the list. We've now been married for five years. What's funny about this story is that the reason my friend's wife put this woman at the top of her list is that the woman had sent her a letter telling her about Social Network Parties and asking for introductions. So, even though I don't like parties, I met my wife as a result of one!"

Joan: Joan had a strong sense of independence and had been single since the break-up of a bad marriage in her teens. She worked as a hairdresser for a chic salon and, although she loved her job, she eventually became unhappy in her love life. "I just kept meeting losers," she admitted. "It was hard to meet someone at work because most of my clients were women. So, after work, I would go to whichever singles' bar was the current 'in' spot and check out who was there. But, somehow, some way, my antenna always found the least available guy in the crowd. He'd either be married or pining away for someone else or a Don Juan who never would settle down. My forehead must have had a neon sign on it which said 'Afraid of commitment' because that is just who would catch my eye.

"Then I turned 31. Somehow, my 30th birthday was not too bad. Lots of friends were there to celebrate and although I was prepared to feel bad, I didn't. Then came 31 and bam! Perhaps it's because my best friend got married that year or maybe it's just that reaching 31 means you are on your way to 40, but I got scared. I remember thinking, 'I'll never find the right guy. Never.' So, I stopped going to singles' bars. Cold turkey, I just stopped. Why bother when all you are doing is wasting your time? But, after staying home for six weeks, I began to miss them. Picking up guys had been my only hobby, if you know what I mean. When that was gone, I had nothing to replace it. So, do you know what I did? Even I couldn't believe it at the time. I went to see a minister. I hadn't been to church since I had left home, but somehow it felt like the right thing to do.

"He was great. He suggested I join the church's young singles' group. I went to a few of their meetings, but there were so many people, most of whom seemed to know each other, that I didn't talk to anyone. Luckily, the minister noticed this and suggested I join one of the service groups. These are small groups that commit to helping a charity. I joined one which visited a rest home. It was really great. We even went on Christmas day, and it was the best Christmas I've ever had. But no one in my service group seemed to be permanent partner material, and I didn't have the time to join more than one group since I work all of Saturday which is when most of the other groups met.

"Then, I heard about Social Networking. I thought, 'What a great idea! But I don't need to solicit the names of quality people. There are over 300 singles in this organization. Why not adapt the method to get to know more of these people?' So, I approached the minister and told him my idea about having small dinner parties to help people meet each other easily. He agreed. We called them 'Dinners for eight.' People were asked to be hosts and hostesses and then seven names were drawn at random to be invited to each dinner. All the dinners were potluck. I met my husband at the seventh dinner I attended."

Perry: Perry is a busy man who runs a construction company and often works seven days a week. When he heard about Social Networking, his first reaction was, "I just don't have the time to do all this work." But, the holidays were approaching and the prospect of spending them alone was not appealing, so he decided he'd figure out some way to host a dinner. He explains, "I was single and my work was booming. In fact, at that time, I had more money than time. It's true. I didn't even have enough time to spend my money. So, I decided why not find someone who had more time than money and share the load. Well, I didn't have to go far from home. My younger brother had just broken up with his girlfriend. He was still in school and, with vacation coming up, had some time on his hands. We composed a funny letter about two lonely brothers. We put it in the form of a song, a variation on 'Brother, Can You Spare a Dime?' Then we decided to send out tapes instead of regular letters. He did all the work. I paid the bills. You would not believe the results! We met the neatest people. That was three years ago. We are both married now. Believe me, excess money is certainly no longer a problem!"

Social Networking or some well thought out variation have a broad appeal to singles of all ages. Whether you are recently divorced, widowed, single for a long or short time, *Social Networking offers a great way of gaining introductions to a group of people you might be unable to reach otherwise*. Yes, they take time and energy to set up and execute even if you choose to organize a gathering that's a bit different from the standard variety. But testimonial after testimonial verifies that they are more than worth the effort. So many men and women have found their permanent partners after hosting or just attending a Social Network Party, we feel confident in recommending that you can do the same. Get creative and start organizing your first special gathering for the kind of people you want to know. You'll make some companionable new friends and, who knows, one of the guests at one of your parties could be just the right partner for you.

Questions and Exercises

Clarifying Your Thoughts and Feelings: If you believe that you cannot host a Social Network Party as described in the previous chapter, but you have decided to take more control of your social life, do this first: really clarify for yourself what it is that causes you to avoid moving forward. No adequate place? Fear? Limited funds? What?

If, after thinking about it, you are absolutely convinced that Social Networking would not work for you, then so be it. Skip to the next chapter and good luck. Otherwise, proceed.

Brainstorming Ideas: Now that you know exactly what holds you back and you are sure that you are being honest with yourself, do some brainstorming as to how to proceed under these circumstances. Brainstorming with another person might trigger more ideas, but it can be done all by yourself. Remember to follow the rules. Don't censor your ideas. Just jot them down as fast as you think of them. Don't evaluate your ideas for usefulness until you feel spent and can't think of anything else. Do let yourself get a little wild and crazy. Getting a bit "far out" can sometimes break a boundary in your thinking and open up a very practical idea. You can start with any of the ideas mentioned in this chapter that appeal to you.

Next look at your brainstorming ideas and select any that you believe you really can do.

Narrow these down to your two or three best ideas and make your choice as to what will work best for you.

Plan Your Party: Set out your preliminary plan for your very first Social Network Party.

Whom are you going to involve to work with you (your core group)? You'll need to make it clear to these people what you think you can actually do and what you would like them to do.

Who will to be your search-helpers? (You should already have this list.) Your core group may have additions.

Where is it going to be held? Who will check this place out?

What is it going to be like? What will be special about it?

Who will do the pre-screening of possible guests?

What is your target date for your gathering?

Begin to see yourself in your mind's eye having a wonderful time and being well-rewarded for your work. What are some key elements that you "see" that are important for you to do to make your Social Network party variation a happy success?

Put some care and effort into your planning and preparations. Remember that chance does indeed favor the prepared mind!

Chapter 9

Step 5:
Letting Go

❤ ── ❤

When we have done our best, we should wait the result in peace.
                                                    J. Lubbock

Here's a summary of what we've covered so far:

Step 1: "Heal Any Wounds" is about uncovering self-defeating habits and learning the direction you need to take for positive change. It's about giving up unsuccessful patterns and putting successful ones in their place.

Step 2: "Know What You Want" urges you to clarify what you want and set appropriate, healthy goals. It's about taking responsibility for your personal standards and the quality of your life.

Step 3: "Be What You Seek" is about transformation of self and becoming a whole person in preparation for becoming half of a team. It is about completing yourself and making yourself an even more attractive being to yourself and others.

Step 4: "Take Charge" encourages you to follow a blueprint for a successful way to meet successful people. Social Networking puts you at the helm of your search. It lets *you* orchestrate whom you bring into your life.

All of these steps involve action, change, responsibility and control. Each takes persistent effort, commitment, hard work and sometimes money.

However:

> after you have done your homework and figured out what might be pointing you in a wrong direction,

> after you feel you are progressing satisfactorily on a new and better path,

> after you have learned ways to put yourself in the right place, at the right time, with the right people,

then it's time to relax, let go and be open to what life has to offer. Relax and let go of all the effort involved in seeking a new partner.

Open yourself to accepting a brand new set of possibilities and some happy synchronicities in your life.

Step 5 Is Different

Why is "letting go" so different? This step doesn't require putting out so much effort. As you may have experienced, we seldom grow when life is rosy. We seem to have to experience pain and have a strong desire to get out of it to push us, to start the search for something better. Haven't you at some time said, "There's got to be a better way!"? It's as if we have to do the preparations, lay the foundation and then empty ourselves in order to leave room for life to fill us up with what is best for us. In fact, at the point that we stop trying to force a certain outcome, somehow the dice land in our favor. But a certain level of consciousness about who and what we are needs to be reached first. As you do your homework, you will release some of the old "stuff" and make room for the new.

Why is it so necessary to take the step of letting go? An interesting theory lies at the very heart of many religions, spiritual paths and philosophical systems. It has to do with growth and consciousness. We talked earlier about Life being a great teacher. The process of solving life's problems enriches us and forces us to continue to unfold. It forces us to examine uncomfortable feelings, distorted beliefs, negative behaviors and erroneous decisions. It forces us to dig deep inside ourselves and reach beyond ourselves. It fosters our spiritual growth and development. It changes our perception of the reality we once thought true. It encourages us, as Joseph Campbell quotes a sage, to engage in "joyous participation in the sorrows of the world." Life also constantly reminds us of the limitations of our ability to control everything and everyone. We can only be in control of ourselves. Attempts to do otherwise backfire. Certainly this knowledge can be very frustrating, but it also can be reassuring and, most importantly, liberating. Perhaps accepting the limitations of our control—releasing them to the winds—opens up a panorama of blessings that we would not appreciate or even be aware of otherwise.

At our core is a joyous spirit pushing to be expressed in the world. In order to be a permanent partner, you must never stop fostering your own personal growth or the growth of your loved one. Failure to do so results in becoming stale and eventually stagnant. Just as stagnant water breeds disease, a stagnant relationship is the breeding ground for an unhealthy, festering encounter of the worst kind. Failure to grow in response to the challenges of life is like a disease. Instead of being true permanent partners, we engage in hollow accommodations that easily crumble when assaulted by life's challenges. As we mentioned in the introduction, there are common threads that run through the fabric of every permanent partnership we examined. When you have taken the four previous steps, you will have had practice in many of the very skills that give these threads their texture.

Expect the Unexpected

It is difficult to pinpoint exactly what occurs when someone stops fighting commitment and becomes genuinely receptive. One thing is certain: When self-love gains a foothold in the psyche, loving things start to happen—especially in a psyche that previously has felt undeserving of love. Even the smallest amount of self-love is fertile ground for more love to grow. It's like the principle of fanning a small flame so a great bonfire can come into being. People who love and respect themselves send a signal to others that they are indeed lovable and worthy of respect. You have probably noticed that much of what we send out, both good and bad, comes back sometimes tenfold. It's as if we have to send parts of ourselves out into the world, maybe see them as in a mirror for the first time (as we do in projection), and then bring them back in a happier, more honest form.

After working on inner growth, either through the previous four steps or by some other means, we reach a place where we no longer need to learn through repetitions of old patterns. Somehow, the lessons we needed to learn have sunk in. We've created the space for something new. It's time to let go and be open to the unexpected.

Every person in our study found their treasure at the end of their journey. But, *hardly anyone found their prize in the guise they expected.* That is why it is necessary to release the old feelings and beliefs and be open to accept the unanticipated—the joyous surprise. Many of the people we spoke with described this fifth step as a transition from a state of seeking to one of relaxation and receptiveness. After a period of active pursuit of a goal, the searcher stops and allows the goal to materialize.

Strange and wonderful things really do happen. They are the serendipities and synchronicities that focus us on life's mysteries, often defying our rational selves. The passage from taking charge to letting go and becoming receptive can be difficult. In some ways, it seems the opposite of what you have been previously asked to do. All we can say is, for whatever the reasons, this seems to be the way it works. We may not be able to explain exactly why but we have a perspective.

One Perspective

As mentioned earlier, most of us have learned to view ourselves as limited. We are lacking. We need something or someone "out there" in order to make us whole and happy. We can feel frustrated and stifled by these limitations. We accepted this view of ourselves as if it were some kind of truth which never changes. Instead of seeing ourselves as the joyous, talented, loving creatures we could be, we settled for much less.

In early life, most of us accepted the outer world's view of us as if it were real. What we heard, saw and felt guided our decisions about our possibilities. Once we made these decisions, we proceeded to reinforce them in order to keep our world in order. We began to live up to what was expected of us. The way we learned to think about ourselves began to create our reality. "For as he thinks within himself, so he is."[1] If we learned to think we were unlovable, we started to act unlovable. If we learned to think we were stupid, we started to act stupid. When our experience of ourselves becomes painful enough, we are driven to seek something better. The "inner work" becomes changing these erroneous perceptions—the distorted way we learned to think about ourselves and our possibilities. When we begin to see it that way, inner growth becomes a shedding, a *letting go* of all we've clung to that gives us pain and makes us unhappy. Inner growth is peeling away old beliefs, distortions and emotions that cloud over and hide our real possibilities. To get to our core, we need to remove the layers one by one and let our "real Self" shine through. We need a new, limitless view—a view that doesn't set unrealistic boundaries on who we can be, what we can do, and on our inner peace and happiness. T. S. Eliot puts it poetically in *The Four Quartets*:

> *We shall not cease from exploration*
> *And the end of all our exploring*
> *Will be to arrive where we started*
> *And know the place for the first time.*

In a humbling way, Ivonne, Nora and Susan experienced the serendipities of inner work. When they let go and became open to new possibilities, the unexpected happened.

Ivonne: Ivonne, a research technician who is adept at taking charge of situations and keeping track of details, took the first three steps in a fairly conventional way. As part of this process, she got in touch with the importance of being honest with herself and others. She had not been either in her first marriage, and she resolved not to make the same mistakes again. Her experience of being open to what life brings took a strange twist.

A miserable marriage, an unhappy divorce and a long struggle with alcoholism paved the way for Ivonne's readiness for change. She chose the Extra-Strength Dose cure, entered into a 12-step recovery program and spent five years getting her life and priorities in order. During this time, it became clear to her that she wanted to be sober, to live her life with honesty and integrity and be happily married. She knew what she wanted. In fact, she knew this in great detail since that was her nature. She worked hard at being what she sought and continued to practice such attributes as honesty rather than denial and little white lies. About three years into her recovery, she decided it was time to start a social life. It was a struggle. As a single mother with a demanding job, she had neither the time nor energy to seek a mate. "At the end of the day, I barely had enough energy left to make dinner and spend some time with my kids. I certainly did not feel like dressing up and going out to mingle with a group of strangers in hopes of finding my Prince Charming.

"But, somewhere in my brain was the idea that the only place I would ever meet a guy was at a bar or a singles' party, so, for a couple of years, I forced myself to go. By the time my shift was near the end, I was so grumpy that all I could think about was getting home. Once I got home, I would be impatient with my kids. They needed so much attention and I was hard-pressed to give it. After all, I was trying to get myself dressed and ready to go out for the evening. Going out meant getting home late.

"Then one day, it dawned on me! In fact, it happened at an AA meeting. The subject was looking at how we exert our own will trying to force a specific outcome to happen in a specific way. It just doesn't always work that way. You have to do the best you can to be ready to take advantage of what comes along and then give up control. That's really hard for me; I want to control everything. But hard as it was, I did it. I gave up trying to find a mate in the way I was formerly convinced was the only way. I relaxed. I decided my mate was out there, but I would have to trust that I would find him without shortchanging other important aspects of my life. My kids needed me and so did my job. I just couldn't spend so much time and effort at singles' functions. I didn't stop looking. I didn't give up my dreams. I just accepted the fact that my permanent partner might not be waiting at the exact location I pictured.

"Then it happened. Just two weeks after I made that discovery, I met my husband, although 'met' is the wrong word to use in this case.

Can you believe it? I actually had known him for several years; he was my shift relief! He told me he had been convinced I hated him because I was so short-tempered every time he came on duty. Then, when I slowed down and became less impatient, he realized I might be a decent person. He remarked that I looked and seemed more relaxed. And when I explained to him why, the door opened wide for a wonderful, amazing conversation about how hard it was to find a nice person to date. One thing led to another and we now have been happily married for over 15 years."

Ivonne's potential partner was right under her very nose all the time, but she had to stop striving before she could see him. She had to get her head out of the past and the future and see what was in front of her right now.

"Step 5: Letting Go," entails giving up control and allowing "luck" to help you out. Luck comes in many forms and wears a variety of costumes. But luck implies good fortune. The following story about how one couple met was so unbelievable that if we had we seen it in a movie, we would have dismissed it as untrue. Yet, it was very true and, in retrospect, even funny.

Nora: Nora's hard work and talent had earned her an important and demanding job in the media. One day at a monthly staff meeting she took notice of a good looking fellow. When he got up to speak, it was clear that in addition to being good looking, he was also funny and bright. This intrigued her. Although she occasionally dated, she had been focusing on her career and had not been seriously involved with anyone for some time. She had recuperated from an unhappy divorce, had learned from her mistakes, and was starting to feel ready to love again. As part of her search, she had asked a few acquaintances, including her advisor, for introductions to eligible men, but no one had seemed just right.

Now she was happy she had shared something so personal with her advisor because it made it easy to ask for information about this attractive man she had just noticed. She was told his name was Kevin, but although he was single and extremely nice, he wasn't available. In fact, he was living with someone. When Nora heard this, she mentally put him out of her mind. She continued to see him at meetings and thought that once or twice he smiled at her, but that was the limit of their interaction.

Then one day, a letter arrived in her inter-office mail. It was not only a love letter, but it was also in verse. It mentioned seeing her periodically at meetings and, to her astonishment and delight, was signed "Kevin."

Nora was ecstatic and instantly began to suffer the pangs of infatuation. Her best friend warned her not to act precipitously or against her better judgment, but Nora couldn't contain herself.

She composed an immediate, poetic response admitting the infatuation, signed it "N," and pushed it through the half-open window of Kevin's car. Then she waited, and waited and waited. But no response was forthcoming.

A week passed and depression began to settle in. Then Nora received a puzzling phone call from a man at the studio she barely knew and didn't feel comfortable around. He asked if he might visit her at home that evening. She was so surprised, it took her awhile to respond that she was unavailable. Then finally it dawned on her. His name was also Kevin. She had poured her heart out in a love letter and given it to the wrong Kevin!

Another week passed. As she recovered from her embarrassment and disappointment, Nora realized her feelings for "her" Kevin—the Kevin she was attracted to—had not disappeared. After much thought, she decided to confront him and explain the mistaken identity. She figured that in order to move on emotionally and get over her feelings, it was best to admit she was the one who had left the letter in his car. So she called him, asked to speak to him privately, and confessed her deed, confusion and embarrassment. It was one of the hardest things she had ever done. At first Kevin was surprised and somewhat embarrassed himself. Their next few meetings were a bit awkward. But, when his relationship with his live-in girlfriend ended a month later, he called Nora and they started dating. They were married 18 months later. Both are convinced they would have never found each other if that fateful letter from the wrong man had not brought them together.

Susan: You met Susan in Chapter 5. Her life has been filled with surprises. The first time the unexpected happened to Susan she was a never-married, 31-year-old who was organizing Social Network Parties in conjunction with two other women in her church. Since none of them had a suitable home in which to meet, they arranged to use the church's recreation room for their gatherings. They didn't call them Social Network Parties then but the format was the same: a dinner party for selected singles who hadn't yet met.

Susan was on her way to her third dinner. She arrived so early that the door to the social room was locked. It seemed silly to go home and then come back and she didn't feel like hanging around an empty building. So, she did something which was on her "never" list: she went to a bar that was in the hotel down the street from the church. It was a well-known singles' place and Susan hated places like that.

The bar was fairly empty. In addition to the bartender and a bored looking waitress, there was one customer who came over and introduced himself to her soon after she sat down. Within a short period of time, she knew that in spite of where they were this was a wonderful guy. Ten months later, she and Jeff were married in the very same church that had been the setting for Susan's dinner parties. When people asked how they had met, they would smile and say, "As the result of a church social."

Remember that Susan also had as a life's goal to be financially stable. Attaining financial independence in her own right with her husband, Jeff, cheering her on was another big surprise.

Several years later, Jeff died of lung cancer. Susan was devastated. After a long mourning period, she decided to go through the steps and begin a search for another partner.

The first thing Susan did was volunteer to be a sponsor at a bereavement group which had supported her during her mourning. The group's purpose was to assist in the grieving process. A sponsor is a person who has been through the grieving process and helps a newcomer. In addition, she volunteered to help with several social causes such as lung cancer prevention. After being involved with these activities for awhile, Susan felt comfortable enough socially to start to date.

As she had done many years earlier, Susan teamed with friends and organized Social Network Parties. She met quality men but none seemed quite as wonderful as her lost mate. However, she continued to risk going out in spite of the disappointments each relationship seemed to bring.

One night, Susan had been on a date with a man she knew was not right for her. She cut the date short and drove home feeling very frustrated and somewhat depressed. It had been an awful week. Business was off. Two people had quit. The toilets in her home had backed up and ruined the new carpeting. She had no plans for the weekend. She missed her husband terribly and felt alone, very alone. "Why do I have to go through so much pain," she complained to herself, on the verge of tears. Suddenly she heard a loud crash. On the other side of the highway, a car had smashed into a pole. Susan immediately went for help. She found a phone and called the police. "Whew," she thought later. "It's been a tough week and I feel pretty awful, but things could be a lot worse!"

Two months later, Susan got a call from a woman she had met at one of her dinner parties. The woman said that her next door neighbor had lost his wife in a car crash. He was not ready for Social Networking, but could Susan introduce him to the bereavement group? Susan contacted the man and sponsored him at the group. In disbelief, she learned that his wife had died in the very car crash she had witnessed.

Susan knew from their first meeting that this man was really special. But under the circumstances, she gave him plenty of time to recuperate and heal from his wife's death before allowing a romantic relationship to flourish. They developed a genuine friendship first and progressed to a more intimate relationship when the time was right for him. As Susan said, "Had I not gone through the steps, I would have tried to rush things. Had I not hosted Social Network Parties, I would have never met the woman who ultimately introduced me to this wonderful man. But also, if I had not gone through the experience of losing a mate myself, I would have never had the patience and understanding to survive the often difficult experience of supporting someone else who is experiencing it. So, I don't know if I was 'lucky' in the conventional sense of the word, but I certainly feel fortunate that life conspired to give me just what I needed. There's no question that I was in the right place and right frame of mind to be the right partner for my husband. He truly is wonderful and I can't imagine anyone better suited as permanent partners than he and I. It was hard, but it was worth it. Life certainly takes some strange turns."

Call it "luck." Call it "fate." Believe in it or not. The experience of many people in our study was that letting go of the old and being open for new twists in life played a role in their achieving happiness. But it didn't work without a preamble. For most, the process involved first putting forth maximum effort and then letting go and allowing the results to materialize for them. The old adage, "The harder you work, the luckier you get," seemed to ring true. When we prepare ourselves and then lay judgment or interference aside, the most astounding things can happen. A time will come for you when it's right to be open and allow your cup to be filled. As a cheerful, used-car salesman shared, "Things turn out the best for the people who make the best out of the way things turn out."

ENDNOTE

1. The *Bible*, Proverbs 23:7, New American Standard Translation.

Questions and Exercises

Recalling Your Experiences of Letting Go: This chapter encourages you to do your work, then let go, stop making so much effort, and be open. Just relax a few minutes right now and recall times in your own life when Life itself seemed to have the best answer for you, when preparation and opportunity conspired to create success. Ponder these times. Think about what you did and didn't do. Recall any good feelings that accompanied the events and simply savor them.

Learn to Quiet Your Mind: One important way to get to your inner core is to learn ways to stop the incessant chattering in your brain. We sometimes experience such moments when we are in prayer or meditation. We suggest that you systematically practice quieting your mind. One way to do this is to find a place where it's relatively peaceful where you won't be interrupted and just sit still for 15 or 20 minutes. Clear your mind of thoughts, take a few deep breaths, relax your body, and then take a listening attitude to something very deep inside you. Begin concentrating on your breath going in and out. This helps to keep you focused because you will find your mind tends to be undisciplined and wanders all over the place. Some people like to focus on repeating a word such as "one" or "peace." When you become aware that you are off on a tangent thinking about something else, just gently allow the thoughts to stop without engaging them further and return to focusing on your breath. Think of your thoughts as if they were a bus coming down the street that you notice but let go by and don't board. Doing this twice a day would be optimum. But doing it at all, for any amount of time, is helpful. It's a way to stop the world and get in touch with your true, inner Self.

Chapter 10

Conclusion

Man's mind stretched to a new idea never goes back to its original dimensions.
Oliver Wendell Holmes

Making a decision to commit to sharing your life with another person is rarely an easy one. However, taking the steps we've suggested can move you in a direction that allows you to get much closer to accomplishing your goal: a future with a partner who is in every sense a true partner—caring, loving, honest, committed and *permanent*. You may have some work to do to become a potential partner yourself, so go back over the steps and keep progressing with your own growth. If you haven't done any of the Questions and Exercises, this may be the time to start. See what information and insights you can glean about yourself and set about making your plans for action. Unless you put energy behind your dream, the best of intentions will disappear like the air in a punctured balloon.

The Matching Process puts you at the helm of your search for a person who is suited to share your life's journey. Once you are very clear about where you want to go, you'll know who is best to go with you. And remember, you are also going along on that person's life journey. To meld two lives is an awesome task so don't feel like a failure if you have to repeat or re-evaluate your progress on some of the steps. We all learn at very rates. Some people breeze through these steps having one "aha!" after another. Others take a slower, more methodical and deliberate approach. While you probably know what will and won't work for you, you may need to let an old fable be your guide. The story of the Tortoise and the Hare has survived for generations because of its underlying truths. Take the time you need. The important thing is to get there.

In the introduction, we mentioned that in addition to the five-step Matching Process, we also uncovered additional basic principles to consider when looking for a lasting love. While these principles speak the truth, they seem to go against conventional wisdom. Perhaps they'll mean more to you now.

1. Meeting Potential Partners Is Relatively Easy.

While there are many methods of meeting potential partners, Social Networking has definite advantages. You now know how this system works. Executive search firms could not stay in business if they did not have a reliable, efficient method for locating personnel—the right people for jobs. You can apply all of this expertise to your search for a permanent partner. When you "Know What You Want" (the job description) and can "Be What You Seek" (the candidate profile), you will be able to recognize a permanent partner without difficulty. If you find yourself still drawn to the wrong "candidates," you need to seek more help ("Heal Any Wounds") in order to be fully prepared to "hire" the right person. Social Networking gives you a vehicle for a systematic search that works.

Meeting potential partners is relatively easy but not effortless, and not every Social Network Party will be a rip-roaring success. But, if you keep at them, you will ultimately meet a large number of very interesting new friends and many potential partners. One of these "potentials" may well be your permanent partner. The payoff is worth the effort.

2. Being a Permanent Partner Is Very Challenging.

After reading the previous chapters, you probably have arrived at the same conclusion we have. It takes a sense of urgency about your priorities to maintain a true partnership that is nourishing to both parties rather than toxic to either. The successfully married people with whom we talked stated that it takes an enormous amount of focused attention to ensure that the marriage stays on the right track: deepening, growing, changing, developing. It takes a lifelong commitment to sustain such a partnership. Our experience says that it's much better to put your energies into doing the steps we suggest *before* you make your choice and marry. For example, don't start immediately with Social Network Parties and an active search. If you have relationship problems to clear up, do that first. Get your foundation laid so that you do not become another statistic. Social Networking will introduce you to many new people even if you are not ready to be attracted to someone who is appropriate for you. You want to find your spouse *when you are aware and better prepared* for commitment. Otherwise, you risk repeating old behaviors and putting on the same old show one more time. If relationsickness is not your problem, then by all means go ahead and "Take Charge." More power to you.

3. You Do Not Need to Make Any External Changes to Be More Attractive to Members of the Opposite Sex.

Let's face it. If a fabulous exterior were all it took to be happily married, most Hollywood stars would certainly have a better track record of marital bliss. Several single women reminded us of this fact, "and the woman he married after he dumped me wasn't even pretty!" In fact, there were few perfect-looking physical matches among the successful couples whom we interviewed.

Books and magazines which give you instructions about how to flirt, change your wardrobe, build muscles or re-do your hair in order to attract a mate can be sorely misleading. External changes can be great, but they are only great if they reflect a more appealing "inside" which gives you a sense of well-being which is translated into sustained, increased self-esteem. It is increased self-esteem which becomes attractive not the new shape or hair style. Appearances are important but it is the inner glow which is sustaining. It's very disappointing to get past a pretty face or a good build and find nothing there.

4. You Probably Will Need to Make Significant Internal Changes to Be More Attractive to Yourself.

Internal changes almost always result in increased self-esteem of the kind that endures. When you live in harmony with your deepest values, you will radiate a sense of well-being that is immensely alluring to those around you. You will literally like yourself more because you will feel more "together," more congruent. Aren't you more comfortable around people who like themselves and refrain from putting themselves down? While we don't know exactly how it works, it is as true as it is trite: liking yourself in a healthy way is the very best way to invite others to like you, too.

Spend the time to get in touch with your values and make those adjustments that help you live in concert with them. As we've said before: focus on becoming a whole person before you become half a team. Much marital agony is caused by making our choices backwards. Decide what you want to do and be in your life, get yourself healthy and *then* search for the right person to make the journey with you. Partnerships that nourish the soul are mutual and are earmarked by the qualities of harmony, cooperation, genuine caring and sharing.

Your Legacy

The focus in *Love That Lasts* has been on *you* and that is its main reason for existing. However, you are an important part of a larger society. For those who want to establish a close partnership, being a winner at love looms in importance because it impacts the entire culture in which you live. In this sense, it contributes to your legacy for present and future generations. A true partnership that is free of violence and genuinely supportive of both partners offers a powerful model to friends, family, and, particularly, offspring. Like little sponges, children absorb everything they see, hear, and feel. Whatever healing and happiness you bring to yourself will profoundly affect other people. When you become a model of someone who has overcome difficulty and made a positive contribution, you provide inspiration, foster courage, and light the way for others.

Our most profound growth happens through relationships, with people as well as with the rest of creation. One way to get a handle on what's really important in your life and where your possible regrets might lie, is to imagine yourself as very, very old—110 years old—and somehow knowing that you are experiencing your last day. Just relax, lay back a few minutes and from this perspective, look back on your life as if you were viewing it like a movie.

In going through this experience with literally thousands of managers, executives, and counselees, we found that, from this viewpoint, almost 100 percent experienced regrets about the *people* in their lives. Very few expressed regrets that they didn't spend more time on their jobs. For most of us, relationships with family and friends are the bottom line of life that depends on any love we can muster and share with others. Are relationships easy? Probably not. Are they worthwhile? Of course. The good news is that we can all learn to make our relationships more meaningful, more worthwhile, more fulfilling, and more enduring. If your desires go beyond marriage to a lasting and loving partnership, then devote your time and energy to preparing yourself to pick a winner for your partner. Do this just as eagerly and carefully as you might select the best training ground to prepare yourself for a fulfilling career.

We are not saying that work is unimportant. Whether for pay or not, work gives us a way to experience and express our talents, to push the boundaries of our potential, to discover and re-discover our possibilities, to allow our creativity to flourish and to serve others. But we need to give at least as much of a sense of urgency to our relationships. We need to take time for the people we love, including ourselves.

Entering into a partnership and sharing your journey with another can be frightening, but you *can* have a love that lasts. It's just five steps away.

Appendix A

About the Study and Cases

How do spouses meet each other? Is there a single best way? These are hot questions for many singles. Realizing that there is great interest in this topic, we thought a book was in order. As a consequence, our initial search centered around particularly interesting and unusual ways that couples found each other. The selection of people with whom we talked was at first random and opportunistic. We asked married people to tell us their tales about how they met. Thus, we collected stories from hairdressers, colleagues at work, neighbors, friends of friends, patients waiting to see the doctor, etc. Many of these stories were amazing: in front of the vegetable bins at the supermarket. Funny: wrong names on traffic tickets, mixed up mail, misdialed telephone numbers. Unusual: looking for a book on divorce at the book store. Or unbelievable: a mother setting her son up with a blind date that really worked.

But something happened. As people told us about the ways they met, they also told about their partners and their marriages in general. We became more and more interested in the quality of the relationship—and its permanence—than we were in the genesis of the marriage. People in happy, long-lasting relationships fairly glowed when they talked about their spouses and their marriages. They were at ease in their relationship but never took it for granted. They didn't play games or manipulate each other to get what they wanted. Instead, they worked as a team, a real partnership. It was amazing and inspiring all at the same time. What astonished us at first and then became a beacon was that most had experienced very unhappy relationships or had been through divorce. They had felt hopeless about ever finding a permanent partner.

Then, in some way, they experienced transformation in their lives and became real winners at love and marriage. The stories of their journeys from unhappiness to happiness captured our attention. These people had a lot to share with other hopeful singles. They offered thoughtful help and a step-by-step strategy to people feeling frustrated at love. Our search changed course and redirected itself toward couples who had transcended unhappy relationships and were now happily married as permanent partners. Out of well over a hundred interviews, 50 couples were selected to study in depth. We selected those who had "suffered" through painful relationships and who then, in some way, overcame their relationship problems and found happiness and stability in a long-term commitment.

Those selected met the additional criteria of being married 15 years or longer. Each interview lasted over an hour, was taped, and then analyzed. We tried to get the views of both partners but settled for one when that wasn't possible. It soon began to unfold that there was a definite pattern of steps that they all seemed to have taken. These steps and their wisdom became our focus.

This study was not scientific in the sense of having a control group, having a method of randomized selection, or use of standardized tests. Rather it is based on good listening, intuitive questions, and drawing couples out more completely as patterns began to emerge. It is mainly an exercise in good sense. These people made good sense. Perhaps all their steps will not work the same way for everyone. But their steps held grains of simple wisdom that are worth passing on.

While there are couples representing all parts of the country, a majority were from the western United States. They were between the ages of 36 and 75. All were educated at least through high school. Several had advanced degrees and nearly half were in the professions. However, the range of occupations included nurses, teachers, retail clerks, biologists, realtors, college professors, writers, stock brokers, hairdressers, physicians, homemakers, receptionists, salespersons, economists, accountants, stewardesses, business people, police officers, technicians, attorneys, personnel consultants, pilots, and printers. They represented a wide variety of religious beliefs and levels of commitment to particular belief systems. While Afro-Americans, Hispanics, and Asians were represented, the majority of subjects were Caucasian. We have used quotes to allow people to tell their own stories. In the interest of brevity, we have had to change words and phrases here and there but have attempted to stay true to each persons feelings, style of expression, and message, using their words as much as was practical. (One transcription was 37 pages long!) The names, of course, have been changed to protect people's privacy. In some instances we had to alter occupations so the individuals could not be recognized.

In addition to the people we interviewed, several of the stories told here are from private marriage-counseling practice, particularly in Chapter 2. Their tales best illustrate the deeper, underlying psychological issues that affect our self-perception, our choices, and our behavior. They were too appropriate to leave out.

We are grateful to all of the people who trusted us with their stories.

Appendix B

Making a Contract

A contract is a commitment to yourself (or to someone else) to make a change. You can make a contract to change behavior, feelings, or your perceptions about past experiences or people. It is an act of self-determination that marks a genuine decision.

A good contract should be clear, concise, and direct. It involves the following: 1) a decision to do something about a specific problem; 2) a statement of a clear goal to be worked toward in plain and simple language; and 3) how you will know when the goal has been fulfilled.

To make a contract you must have enough awareness about yourself to know what needs to be developed in you. The statement of the goal should be straight-forward and clear. For example:

Stop acting like a martyr;
Stop putting myself down;
Stop putting others down;
Start listening carefully to people;
Start showing affection;
Start respecting myself.

Your contract might look like this:

I have decided to (your decision) _____

I agree with myself to (goal) _____

I will start (date)_____ and keep track of my progress by
_____ (ways to feedback to yourself your progress).

I will know this contract is completed when _____
(what you expect to be different).

These are things I will do to help myself reach my goal (any support, reminders, rewards for yourself, agreements from others you may need.) _____

Appendix C

Helpful Books
for Special Problems

Bass, Ellen, and Davis, Laura. *The Courage to Heal*. New York: Harper Collins, 1992.

Bloomfield, Harold H. *Making Peace with Yourself*. Toronto: Ballantine Books, 1986.

Bly, Robert. *Iron John: A Book About Men*. Reading, MA: Addison-Wesley Publishing Company, 1990.

Botwin, Carol. *Men Who Can't Be Faithful*. New York: Warner Books, 1988.

Branden, Nathaniel. *How to Raise Your Self-Esteem*. New York: Bantam Books, 1987.

Capacchione, Lucia. *The Well-Being Journal*. North Hollywood, CA: Newcastle Publishing, 1989.

Cowan, Connell, and Kinder, Melvin. *Smart Women–Foolish Choices*. New York: Penguin Books, 1986.

Forward, Susan. *Betrayal of Innocence: Incest & Its Devastation*. Los Angeles: JP Tarcher Publishing, 1978.

Halpern, Howard M. *How to Break Your Addiction to a Person*. New York: Bantam Books, 1982.

Harms, Valerie. *The Inner Love*. Boston: Shambhala Publishing, 1992.

Hoffman, Ivan. *The Tao of Love*. Rocklin, CA: Prima Publishing, 1993.

James, Muriel, and Jongeward, Dorothy. *Born to Win: Transactional Analysis with Gestalt Experiments*. Reading, MA: Addison-Wesley Publishing Company, 1971, seventy-second printing 1990. New American Library, 1978.

Jongeward, Dorothy, and Scott, Dru. *Women as Winners: Transactional Analysis for Personal Growth*. Reading, MA: Addison-Wesley Publishing Company, 1982.

Keen, Sam. *Fire in the Belly: On Being a Man*. New York: Bantam Books, 1991.

Keirsey, David, and Bates, Marilyn. *Please Understand Me: Character and Temperament Types*. Delmar, CA: Gnosology Books, 1984.

Lerner, Harriet B. *The Dance of Intimacy*. New York: Harper & Row, 1990.

Moore, Robert, and Gillette, Douglas. *King, Warrior, Magician, Lover: Rediscovering the Archetypes of the Mature Male*. San Francisco: Harper, 1990.

Muller, Wayne. *Legacy of the Heart*. New York: Simon & Schuster, 1992.

Nelson, Gertrude M. *Here All Dwell Free*. New York: Ballantine Books, 1991.

Norwood, Robin. *Women Who Love Too Much*. New York: Pocket Books, 1986.

Tannen, Deborah. *You Just Don't Understand Me: Women and Men in Conversation*. New York: Ballantine Books, 1991.

Appendix D

How to Find a Helping Professional

If you decide that professional help is what you need, there are many ways to go about finding the right person for you. We can't stress it strongly enough that this person should be *the right person for you*. This means that you will have to do some shopping around. The relationship between you and your therapist is an important part of the healing, so make sure that relationship is a healthy one.

The best referral is an enthusiastic recommendation from a satisfied client if at all possible for you. Even here, however, we caution that what is right for someone else may not be right for you. Make a judgment in your own behalf after two or three visits. Other good sources are professionals whom you trust—your doctor, professor, attorney, or perhaps your minister, priest or rabbi. They are likely to know local professionals who have good reputations.

Look for someone who has had experience and perhaps specializes in your kind of problems. For example, some professionals specialize in family therapy, some in phobias, some in sex therapy, addictions, abuse, etc. If possible, find the therapist that fits the bill for you. Most states have requirements for credentialing of psychiatrists, psychologists, marriage counselors, and therapists. You need to make sure the person you select is well trained and meets professional standards. Ask for credentials.

There is a difference between psychiatrists, psychoanalysts, psychologists and psychotherapists. Psychiatrists are medical doctors (psychoanalysts are also usually M.D.s) who specialize in mental and emotional problems. Since they are M.D.s, they can prescribe medication. If you think you need medication, you should look for a psychiatrist. The others are trained to deal with emotional problems and disturbances but do not prescribe drugs. However, many have associations with psychiatrists who assist them. It is important that you know enough about your needs to make a good decision. Other than that, it's the person who makes the difference. You want a well-trained, experienced person who is a person of intelligence, insight, warmth and high integrity. Any therapist who invites you to have sex as part of your treatment is breaching a professional standard in a most profound way. If love and/or sexual desire should develop between you and your therapist which you choose to act on, get another therapist.

Resources

Many schools of psychology have their professional organizations. We are mentioning only two here, but your physician can direct you to others.

If you are interested in a therapist who is trained in transactional analysis, you can write for referrals near you: International Transactional Analysis Association, 1772 Vallejo Street, San Francisco, CA 94123   Phone: 415-885-5992

If you are interested in someone trained in the gestalt therapy method, write for a free copy of *The Gestalt Directory*. This directory includes information about each person's training in gestalt therapy and training in other disciplines, academic background, licensing and professional certifications, along with other helpful information. *The Gestalt Directory*, P.O. Box 990, Highland, NY 12528-0990

Other potential sources of referrals include teaching hospitals, university departments of psychology and social work, and local self-help groups. Increasingly, employee assistance programs in organizations offer confidential counseling and referrals. Your local library is a good place to start. You can even check the "Mental Health" section of the Yellow Pages.

Two Useful Sources

The Family Guide to Mental Health (Prentice Hall, 1991) edited by Benjamin Wolman, offers brief descriptions in lay terms of a wide range of treatments and defines various disorders.

The free pamphlet *A Consumer's Guide to Mental Health Services* is available from the Public Health Service, Alcohol, Drug Abuse, and Mental Health Administration, Rockville, MD 20857.

Professional Associations (partial listing)

The American Psychiatric Association offers a series of pamphlets on mental disorders, substance abuse, and how to choose a psychiatrist. Single copies are free. Write to the APA Division of Public Affairs, 1400 K Street, NW, Washington DC 20005.

The American Psychological Association also publishes pamphlets on mental-health problems, as well as lists of psychological associations in your area. Send a self-addressed stamped envelope to 750 First Street, NE, Washington, DC 20002-4242.

The National Association of Social Workers can refer you to a licensed practitioner in your area. Write to them at 750 First Street, NE, Washington, DC 20002; or call 202-408-8600.

The American Association for Marriage and Family Therapy will send you a brochure and list of therapists in your area. Write to them at 1100 Seventeenth Street, NW, 10th Floor, Washington DC 20036; or call 800-374-2638.

Self-Help Groups

The American Self-Help Clearinghouse can direct you to groups in your area. Write to 25 Pocono Road, St. Clares-Riverside Medical Center, Denville, NJ 07834; or call 201-625-7101.

The National Victims Center's INFOLINK program provides a comprehensive, toll-free source of information on over 60 crime and victim-related subjects as well as referral to thousands of service providers across the nation. Call 1-800-FYI-CALL.

Appendix E

Pearls of Wisdom for Conflict Resolution

Studying and practicing this process will give you guidelines for "defusing" conflict and working your way to resolution. Every couple has conflicts. It's how they handle these differences that spells success or failure in a relationship.

Pearl One

When you are ready to level about what's hurting or what seems wrong, don't bring up an issue out of the blue and expect a partner to jump into problem solving. Instead, make an appointment. Say that you have something important on your mind or that something has been bothering you that you need to talk over. Then set a time that you both feel all right about for bringing up the details. Don't pounce. Set the stage for a serious talk and create the mood for interest in problem solving. Patrick and Elayne used this principal well with their rule number one (their 24-hour rule). "This rule is invoked in a special way. We'll introduce a discussion about something like this, 'You know our rule,' and right away that tells the other partner 1) something very sensitive is going to be discussed, and 2) our marriage is strong because we have these discussions. And then we discuss the issue, which many times is irrational—like an irrational fear or seeing what's going on now as if it's some event from the past. This rule is great because nothing builds up. There are no snowballs. We developed that rule early on because I was such a quiet type and would let things fester."

Pearl Two

Take turns talking. Avoid interrupting as much as possible. If need be, tell your partner that you would like five minutes to get through what you have to say before your partner responds. Then show the same courtesy in return. If things get over heated, try to cool them down. Say that you both will have plenty of time to say what you need to say. Encourage the spirit of "Let's get it out on the table and then we'll figure out what is best for our relationship." Don't try to out-shout each other.

Pearl Three

Stick to the issue at hand and resist the terrible temptation to bring up everything that ever went wrong. Such a temptation only demonstrates that no real resolutions happened in the past. Such unfinished business builds up and festers like a boil just itching to break. At the first point of stress all the resentments pour out. If cashing in a long collection of crimes and misdemeanors happens, say, "We may need to talk about that, but, for now, let's stick to this issue until we're satisfied that it's clear between us."

Pearl Four

Express hostile feelings verbally, never physically. State your concerns from your perception. After all, all any of us have is just our perception. Say, "I feel _____ when _____ " rather than an accusative, "You always _____ ." Remember to show dislike for the behavior not for the person. The behavior can change. When questioning, choose "What?" questions over "Why?" questions. "What?" questions can help you gather information. In contrast, "Why?" questions are challenging and tend to trigger defensiveness. Once defensiveness rears its ugly head, discussion deteriorates into a pattern of attack/defense rather than problem solving.

Pearl Five

Listen to each other carefully. Feed back what the other has said to show that you understand the words and especially how the other person feels. (You don't have to agree.) Just make sure you understand your partner and show it. In the heat of what seems like a battle, keep your eye on what you are trying to accomplish. You want to understand your partner and to make yourself understood. However, if things get too hot, ask for time out to settle down and think things through. But don't create unfinished business. Make your next appointment to resume your discussion.

Pearl Six

Never use abusive language or name calling. It doesn't pay to lower self-respect and self-esteem. Memories of hurtful language linger in our heads long after the event. They are very hard to forgive and forget.

Pearl Seven

Come to some sort of conclusion after understanding has been accomplished. Don't do more than is needed. For example, many times a partner simply wants to be heard, to be understood, and doesn't want solutions or rescuing. Sometimes the issue is between you and your partner and you need to come to a compromise, an agreement, or get some competent outside help. Do whatever is appropriate to the situation. State your understanding, apologize sincerely if an apology is in order, negotiate a resolution with which you both can live, decide on the next step. Complete whatever needs to be done to clear the air and put the issue to rest.

Pearl Eight

Attempt to end on a positive note with a positive gesture. Verbalize how important it is to talk things over. Give each other strokes for facing a problem and deciding what to do about it. The release of anger and resentment unblocks affection. Show your affection with a caring touch. Talk over what made your leveling session work so well.

Remind yourselves that a good relationship is strong enough to take the bumps and many times is strengthened by these bumps. A diamond is born out of heat and pressure.

About the Authors

Dr. Dorothy Jongeward *has authored or co-authored eight successful books, including the 4 million best seller,* Born to Win *and* Women as Winners. *She is an internationally prominent management consultant and a licensed marriage, child and family counselor. She has been with her permanent partner for over 40 years.*

Michele Raffin *earned her M.M.S. at Stanford and has been a computer company vice-president, lecturer and venture capitalist. She developed the concept of "Social Networking" as a means of finding a husband while handling a demanding work life. She currently writes and lives in California with her husband, four children, four dogs and two house rabbits.*